Sept 20 2003
Matt - I hope you
enjoy this -
Love DAD.

ext**r**eme LANDSCAPE

extremeLANDSCAPE
The Lure of Mountain Spaces

NATIONAL GEOGRAPHIC
ADVENTURE PRESS

WASHINGTON, D. C.

IN ASSOCIATION WITH THE BANFF CENTRE FOR MOUNTAIN CULTURE

Acknowledgments

I am grateful to many who believed in and supported this literary collection celebrating International Year of Mountains. First of all to the remarkable writers and photographers who opened a window to their world of extreme landscape through their essays and images. Kevin Mulroy and Johnna Rizzo of NGS Books embraced this project and nurtured it through to completion. The financial support of our sponsors helped make the dream a reality. The Banff Centre and Mountain Culture team provided me with the quiet time and support to close my office door and concentrate on the words. Anne Ryall was thoughtful and thorough in her translation of the Bernard Amy essay. And once again, project coordinator Paula Rondina was unceasing in her efforts to get it done on time. Thank you all.
Bernadette McDonald

Whiteface Tower, Northern Selkirks, British Columbia PIERRE LEMIRE

a literary celebration ✻ BERNADETTE MCDONALD

IN 1992 MOUNTAIN REGIONS around the world finally came onto the environmental radar screen at the Earth Summit in Rio de Janeiro. During that conference, mountain areas were recognized as important planetary water towers and repositories of biodiversity and cultural heritage. The outcome was a blueprint for sustainable development that placed mountains on equal footing with climate change, tropical deforestation, and desertification as crucial issues that needed to be addressed. It was the country of Kyrgyztan that nominated 2002 as International Year of Mountains (IYM) and the United Nations enthusiastically endorsed it.

This book is a literary celebration of International Year of Mountains by writers whose passion for those extreme landscapes fuels their creativity. The journey from the Earth Summit to IYM to a book celebrating extreme landscapes was circuitous, long, and always interesting.

At the Mountain Culture division of The Banff Centre we have been working on mountain cultural and environmental issues since the Rio Summit. During that time I have received a lot of questions about the word "culture." Does it mean a high-level body of creative work, does it refer to indigenous cultures found in mountain areas, or is it simply a nice way of describing the tribal gathering of climbers and adventurers that assemble in Banff each year for the mountain festivals? When we use this word "culture" we mean people—communities and individuals—who are shaped by mountain landscapes and who, in turn, affect those mountain places. We believe that mountain people all over the world have many things in common—their respect for the landscape, their relationship to a dramatic and sometimes tough place to live, environmental issues and economic problems, and their sense of being inspired and nurtured by the grandeur of mountains.

When I was at the United Nations on December 11, 2001, to be part of a special assembly of the UN to launch IYM, I was struck again by the interconnectedness of that global mountain community. In addition to being inspired and encouraged by this gathering, I became excited about doing something special in this year.

And so, to mark International Year of Mountains, we decided to mount a summit meeting in Banff, Alberta. This meeting would bring together the best and the brightest from the mountain world.

We would include scientists, archaeologists, painters, vertical and native dancers, ethnobotanists, writers, and musicians. They would come to Banff for a summit called "Extreme Landscape: Challenge and Celebration." And they would come together in October 2002 to debate issues that were important to mountain communities as well as to celebrate the inspirational value of this dramatic mountain landscape.

As a legacy of IYM and the Banff Summit, this book was created. The themes of the summit debate form the core of this book: essays that touch key issues such as cultural diversity, consumerist approach to landscape, corporate responsibility, inspirational values, spiritual importance, and political reality.

Some argue that mountain experiences must be earned. Others look for easy access to alpine landscapes and are more consumptive in their approach. When we reshape an extreme environment to suit our needs, we lose the ability to experience it on its own terms. And the value of that landscape may become compromised by our ability and willingness to reshape it.

Extreme environments produce subtle physiological changes in the peoples who live in them. But do these landscapes reshape how we think and feel? Some would argue that humankind's thirst for adventure has its roots in our ancestors' experience of extreme environments and that these environments continue to shape human psychology. One cannot help but note the number of mountainous war-torn areas in the world today and speculate on the influence of that landscape on the psyches of those who inhabit those high, barren places.

Extreme landscapes are increasingly important economically; they fuel a burgeoning outdoor industry. At the same time, they are storehouses for essential natural resources, from fossil fuels to clean water. As the extraction of these resources accelerates and as more and more people flock to mountain places in search of adventure, the corporate responsibilities of those who profit from extreme landscapes increase, but their response is not consistent and, as a result, is not sustainable.

Extreme landscapes ultimately shape the people who inhabit them. The severity of the landscape, living conditions, and climate all contribute to the traditions, language, and survival skills unique to each area. We share in the richness of this cultural diversity through language, stories, images, and knowledge. Sadly, in the process of learning more, we may actually be threatening that which is priceless.

Artists, poets, musicians, and writers have been inspired by extreme landscape since the days of cave paintings, resulting in some of the most memorable examples of creativity imaginable. And at a higher level, mountains symbolize spiritual values. Mountain landscapes around the world have a huge impact on our lives: economically, recreationally, environmentally, culturally, and as an inspiration that fuels our creative and physical dreams.

Each of the authors in this collection is a specialist: a scientist, ethnobotanist, mountaineer, philosopher, or photographer. Each has focused on particular mysteries and issues of extreme landscapes and each of them draws creative inspiration from the high peaks and icy expanses of some of the wildest terrain imaginable.

The eloquent responses by the authors of this book are living proof that mountains are a truly inspirational landscape—surely a landscape that is worth celebrating and protecting. This literary legacy is not meant to represent a conclusion to

IYM but rather an important reminder that each individual has the opportunity and responsibility to tread lightly in extreme landscapes.

introduction

the peak of humility ✳ TERRY TEMPEST WILLIAMS

MOUNTAINS INSPIRE OUR HIGHEST SELVES. Wildness is a mirror that reflects how domesticated we have become. When we encounter mountains in wild places we experience the peak of our own humility. Whether we are standing at the summit or paying respects from below, we are flushed with awe. Perhaps this is the beginning of religion.

George Schaller writes, "Mountains are said to be the abodes of distant gods, the unreachable metaphors for life...they become intimate, offering communion and unity with the natural world." To see a mountain in the distance, how it breaks the horizon line and draws your thoughts upward, to contemplate its beauty, to hold its image in your heart as it takes possession of you like a lover, to plan one's ascent, to begin the journey—each step toward the mountain, up the mountain becomes the point of communion. What we learn is this: The mountain keeps its own counsel; it forever remains a mystery; its power is omnipresent.

The essays in *Extreme Landscape: The Lure of Mountain Spaces* articulate some of the mysteries explored in wild country. Each writer has chosen to share his or her own spiritual geography through the stories that have shaped their character. And all of these contributors are human beings of extraordinary character. They are fearless because they have come face to face with fear, be it an avalanche, subzero temperatures, or the unpinning and refastening of their own minds in extreme landscapes. Death is the acceptance of their passionate lives. They are writers with presence because they have stood in the presence of the magnificent and bowed their heads in respect. They are modern-day heroes because they have committed their lives to the journey of adventure and they return home with stories that remind us who we are and who we live among.

"Sharing stories," writes Chris Rainier, "has been a human trait since we began our search for resources across the landscape…the desire to pass along the wisdom that lies deep in all of our souls is the catalyst for the survival of our spiritual being. These tales were profoundly influenced by the contours of this rugged and primordial landscape…."

"What we have lost in the West is the relevance of telling stories to our everyday lives," Rainier continues. "What we have gained is the illusion that we have conquered nature and tamed the extreme landscape of the planet."

Another myth.

We can begin to live differently, not a "going back to nature" but a going forward with a compassion toward life. Gretel Ehrlich tells a story of traveling to Greenland where the "ice cap is a light...that sits atop the world." She travels by dogsled, "a platform for viewing the world," a world very different from her own.

"Conversely, consciousness exists everywhere and in everything. The Inuit know that animals understand everything we do and that we can understand them. Once, we all spoke the same language. What outsiders routinely describe as the Arctic's desolate waste is really a hospitable place full of animals and spirits, voices and stories. The four months of sunlight and the four of darkness is a kind of generosity in which the imagination and the weather can become unanchored. By comparison, our continual and repetitive alteration of day and night is bewildering."

Point of view. Different landscapes. Different languages. All offering tribes a unique way of seeing and defining community. This is the richness of both geographic and cultural diversity. And this is what we are losing in this era of globalization. One world with one language that says we have one value: economic growth. What we don't hear is how this monolithic monetary point of view is at the expense of cultural and ecological health dependent on diversity. "Nature loves diversity," Yvon Chouinard reminds us. "Nature hates an accumulation of anything in one place. It doesn't like cities or mono crops like entire forests of Douglas fir, salmon farms, or endless fields of cotton. A business should grow by diversifying."

Almost without exception, each of the essays in this anthology elucidates how we are losing a diversity of languages and landscapes at our own peril as a species. Landscape shapes culture. Lose the land, lose the culture. It is a simple equation in complicated times. Reinhold Messner says it straight, "What is now at stake is the protection of mountain areas as living space." "Language is a root, not a branch," writes Dermot Somers.

Wade Davis tells four stories rooted in British Columbia, Peru, Australia, and the sands of the Kalahari, home to the San Bushman. He says, "The disappearance of an ancient way of life, morally inspired and inherently right, represents a loss to all humanity....Together the myriad peoples of the world comprise the repertoire with which we will chart a way through the next centuries."

Barry Lopez writes, "A central task facing modern Western cultures is to redefine human community in the wake of industrialization, colonialism and...the forcing power of capitalism...by turning nature into scenery and commodities, we may have cut ourselves off from something vital.... We can't any longer take what we call 'nature' for an object. We must merge it again with our own nature."

Call it a new geography of home and hope. William McDonough and Michael Braungart take these ideas and ground them in the design of our daily lives. The extreme landscape of Everest becomes the extreme landscape of a Kmart parking lot. "Seeing hope in the extremities of the human world begins with our perception of landscape." Enter two more words for discussion alongside diversity: imagination and restoration.

If we can honor the wild in all its diversity, if we can truly act with respect and restraint for all life forms in our definition of community, we will also be honoring the power and beauty of civilization. We can bow to the cultures that have learned to live in harmony with nature, listen to the grace note of interdependence they still hold. Rather than destroy their forests and baptize their children in the name of Christianity and capitalism, we can listen, encourage, and support their struggle to survive in place.

The wisdom of these explorers on the page and in the world is that they have seen these indigenous people in the context of the wild places that have formed them, shaped them, inspired and nurtured them. They have watched the politics of China betray Tibet, they have felt the heat in the wake of deforestation in Brazil and Peru that has left tribal people exposed and vulnerable. These writers, entrepreneurs, and mountaineers have also felt the holes in their hearts, knowing what has been bled out of them by the consumptive cultures we are a part of. We are all complicit in the demise of the wild.

We are in transition from a nonsustainable world to a sustainable one. We are hungry for new stories that can offer us a way to live more fully in place like a tight, strong rope that will hold our weight while we figure out our next move. We are searching for new terrain, not necessarily on mountain tops, but within our own souls that will allow us to find a generosity of spirit, a wildness of the heart that is brave and bold. Making alterations within our own lifestyles that are mindful of others and our impact on the land can become gestures of love—not loss.

When I began reading these essays written with the intention of honoring mountains and the lure of mountain spaces, I did not anticipate that the writers would take me on this path of evolutionary thinking. I thought they would be stories of what they did where and with whom. That each piece would instead honor the sacred rights of a mountain, a forest, a river, a bear, a salmon, and the human beings who live in the midst of these ecological communities, is a testament to the morality of the wild and the altruism it fosters in the name of survival.

The stories held inside *Extreme Landscape* are stories of survival, revelations of how small we are and how large we might become.

North of Disko Bay, Arctic Ocean, west coast of Greenland PIERRE LEMIRE

we called it the attic ✳ GRETEL EHRLICH

WE CALLED IT THE ATTIC, not the Arctic, and laughed at how the ice made a mockery of our fragile bodies. It was May 1991, and I'd flown to Resolute, Northwest Territories, to write about Brendan Kelly, a seal biologist I had met in Fairbanks on a wintry night when the temperature dipped to 82°F below zero. In that viselike grip of cold we agreed to meet again at his field station in the Canadian High Arctic where he was doing DNA work on ringed seals. Cornwallis Island was low, gravelly, and bare, and the weather was stormy. Brendan came for me on his snowmobile.

We traveled west toward Griffith Island for more than an hour. The ice and the sky were a watery skin that was part heaven and part Earth; we were two gulls flying between. Leads in the ice were black, equatorial bands that lashed the waist of the Arctic like sealskin thongs. I say the waist because we were in the center of things, perched above Parry Channel, held between Devon Island to the east and Bathurst Island to the west, with the north magnetic pole just a few miles away. We camped on the frozen ocean in a heated, insulated parcol with two solar panels that kept five laptops and my portable CD player buzzing with the sound of seals diving, as well as Sibelius tone poems, Bach, and Jackson Browne in our ears.

Brendan's two black Labs that he'd flown in from Alaska helped find the seals in their *allus*, or breathing holes. Brendan said his dogs could smell a seal two miles away. Without them we would have roamed the sea ice helplessly. He trapped the seals in nets, pulled them onto the ice, drew blood, and fastened "pingers" that would allow him to track the seals during their dives.

Days when the sun was out, I lay on the sled wrapped in furs, sunbathing on a wide floor of ice. Ice was time. Ice was light. Light was the passage the smooth body made between two islands where no moon traveled in spring. Light equaled the time it took to leap from winter's black sky, where the moon was only a peephole, into the blank brightness.

Time was ice thickening so deep I could not dig down to water. Then, as the weeks went by, it became water that rose to our knees. Ice plus time equaled spring breakup, and time plus light produced the blackness that came before this season and the blackness to come.

All day was all night. We caught seals, roamed the ice, cooked food, lay on caribou skins, drank wine from a box, laughed at the dogs. Light was a knife that cut this island into being. We looked and looked at the horizon. It cuffed our feet as the sun circled our heads. Where the ice shelf breaks off, what begins?

The day the storm came, our tent turned into a lung. Moaning and breathing, collapsing and refilling as we tried to keep it from going down. Everything outside the tent vanished. Smaller tents blew away; the food cache was buried deep, and the snowmobiles. Radio contact with the scientists at the Polar Continental SHELF Project—a research station—was gone. The wind blew a steady 65 knots. For three days we were the island; for three days we lived inside the storm's shaking hands. "What will happen if the tent blows away?" I asked Brendan. "We'll die," he said. All we could do was wait. Hours and days became one hour, one moment. Then, in the cacophony, I heard voices: Everything talked; the walls of the tent talked to the wind and the wind talked to the walls. Our caribou skins began telling us stories about the ring seals that swam under us, about how they climbed into a breathing hole and became a human child. Everything dead talked about everything living, and everything living—including the two of us and the two dogs—talked to the dead in voices that sounded hollow. Even the whale's jawbone resting against a house in Resolute Village talked so loudly we could hear it way out on the ice, and the polar bear skins walked through the storm as if they could see, giving their eyes to the storm.

When it stopped, everything went flat. An Inuit friend of Brendan's from the village came to check on us. He roared up on his snowmobile, stopped in front of our bedraggled tent, and smiled, then roared away, never saying a word. That afternoon, while we were going for a walk, an Eider duck flew over. It was the first sign of spring. We walked a long way out on the ice toward Griffith Island, saw where a polar bear had eaten a seal, saw fox tracks, and those of the *ukaleq*, the Arctic hare, but no other signs of life. "Where do people go when they blow away?" I asked. "The Arctic has its own heaven," Brendan told me.

Farther out between grounded floes of ice, the frozen ocean began melting into cerulean ponds. Blue dotted the white expanse. The horizon in every direction bent its white lip down, drowning in silver. We caught more seals, drew blood, attached pingers, dug out our food cache and snowmobile, and steadied our listing tent. Then it was June. Two weeks later, a ship plowed through the ice where our tent had been: The white floor that had held us since had turned to water.

Once I'd been to the Arctic and felt its bite, I was never the same again. It had been true for Brendan and now it was true for me. But if I wanted to see what was left of traditional hunting and living, I'd have to go to northern Greenland, Brendan told me, where travel was still by dogsled and hunters wore skins.

Two years later, I journeyed to Greenland, the biggest island in the world, 95 percent of which is covered by ice. I traveled alone with no plan of where to go, how to communicate, how to learn more about life on the ice. On the twin from Baffin Island to Nuuk, Greenland, a couple—OleJorgen and Ann (he was Inuit, she from the Faroe Islands)—befriended me. I was carrying a volume of notes by the celebrated ethnographer-explorer Knud Rasmussen—the national hero of both Greenland and Denmark. We talked of him (OleJorgen is related to Rasmussen), of his seven expeditions around Greenland and across the polar north, and by the time we reached the shores of Greenland, they insisted I travel north with them to see "the real Greenland," where people travel by dogsled and kayak, wear skins, and, in some villages, live a subsistence hunting life. My eight years of travel in Greenland had begun. A friend, John Perry Barlow, wrote: "I looked down on Greenland from a plane where you had gone and beheld a rim of coastal crags containing a bowl of immense white purity, ice several thousand feet deep. Slow rivers could be seen snaking from its heart, calving pale islands from their mouths into the sea."

Greenland is mountainous, composed of some of the oldest rock in the world, and wears its hard hat of ice pulled down into canyons, all the way to the ocean. It has the most productive glaciers in the world, and the ice cap is a light that sits atop the world. Its presence is always felt. Walk out on the ice and look up; it is its own mountain piled on top of a mountain-island of rock. The people who have lived on its rocky fringes for 5,000 years are in a long transitional phase between ice age living and some miasma of modernity that will change them.

The Inuit occupy the greatest lineal distance of any single racial or linguistic group in the world. Having come from Siberia, across the Bering land bridge between 30,000 and 12,000 years ago, they continued on across Alaska, taking what we know as the Northwest Passage across Arctic Canada and, 5,000 years ago, leaped from Ellesmere Island across 36 miles of ice to Greenland. They not only have survived in this harshest climate in the world, but also have thrived. Their culture is rich and unique, having flourished in relative isolation for thousands of years.

A hunting culture is more than atavistically searching for food and gulping it down when you get it. It is a full moon with many aspects—cultural, spiritual, physical, and biological—and requires a keenness of mind and body, a comprehension of the complexities of animals, village mores, weather, and ice.

After my initial visit, traveling with my new friends Ann and OleJorgen in the summer of 1991, I returned to Uummannaq in the dark time, the winter, and stayed until the sun made its first appearance in February. In order to understand the Inuit mind, I had to experience the dark. Flying north from Illulissat, the ocean was gray flannel, then all ice. Ahead was a wedge of black and we were going toward it, that single ash in which we might burn. Then it came all around us, a deluge of black iron splinters, falling inside us…darkness streamed. I felt as if my eyes had been taken out of my head, or else my face was one eye trying to see anything. No images rose. We seemed to fly with no speed. Then the helicopter rotored down.

I lived in a cold greenhouse where the snow from my boots did not melt. It was bolted to rock on a hill with a view of the harbor and grocery store. All the workings of the village were laid out before me: children playing; hunters coming and going; the local doctor, a Dane who had come to Greenland 27 years before and never gone home. But the workings of the mind foiled by dark soon took interesting routes. Everything external took up residence inside me, and everything inside flew out and dissipated in black air. The sky was a sea that had swallowed us, and the black fjord water was pure india ink, sloshing against vertical black walls. The moon rose between two dihedral buttresses and bounced off the ice cap, then broke free.

In those many weeks of black mornings, middays, and nights, the moon dragged its lamp across ice. And, despite thoughts about Diogenes, I still couldn't distinguish this from that, reminding me that there is only one world, one life, and all sentient beings share in it. Some days I imagined I could lift up the darkness like a stone with a shovel. When that failed, I thought I could pierce it so abruptly, I'd break through to sunlight. Nothing worked. I lay back and relaxed. Sleep came often. I wrote by candlelight and read Rasmussen's notes from the second Thule expedition. The darkness turned soft, almost velvety, like something I could hold on my tongue, and my face turned around backward on my head and I saw a different order of things. Darkness was the arm that held me.

Then the sun came. Just a little cuticle of brightness peeking above the mountains of Nuussuaq Peninsula. We all ran to the top of the village and welcomed it with anorak hoods off, palms held out, faces turned upward. It was the custom to greet the sun this way, for if you did not, you would die within the year.

February is when the light comes back, and by May it is a halo above one's head. There are no hours of twilight, just brightness blasting.

The next summer, I spent a month on Unknown Island, 50 miles north of the island of Uummannaq. Its one village, Illorsuit, faced north into a six-mile-wide fjord and a wall of rock that rose on the other side. The fjord water was ink, the wall was black from meltwater, and all day and all night icebergs drifted by like photographic negatives of the dark mountains beyond. It had been difficult getting there. I arrived by helicopter in Uummannaq with no way to get to Unknown Island. All my friends were off on holiday. I had no luggage—it had been lost—and no place to stay. I wandered around, trying to find a fishing boat going that way. Making myself understood was difficult. I waited in the harbor. Finally, in the evening hours, a boat came in and I was told, in Greenlandic, which I didn't understand, that the man at the helm was from Illorsuit. I ran over to the high-bowed boat as he docked and said the name of the village and the name of the one

English speaker on the island who might be expecting me. He listened, said nothing, then held out his hand to help me aboard. Later, as we sailed out of the harbor into the open sea, I wondered if we were really going to Illorsuit, if he had understood what I said.

We arrived at two in the morning. It was a small bay and the village was a string of small houses on the sand. I had no idea which house belonged to Hans, my contact, nor had I been able to tell him I was coming. I climbed the metal ladder to the dock and wandered slowly through the village. There were dogs chained everywhere, sleds stacked up, skiffs tied up all along the beachfront, a few children playing. The sky was bright, but all was quiet, only small waves slapping the shore. Then I heard a woman's voice. She was motioning to me. I followed her down a path to a yellow house at the end of the strand. Two children ran to me, jumping up and down and saying things I couldn't understand in Greenlandic. Then their father, Hans, a Dane, appeared and said, "We've been expecting you," though it had been months before when we last exchanged letters about my visit. "You must be hungry. I'll make you some toast. I remember that Americans and English like toast...."

That summer, light turned me inside out. There was no privacy. Nothing happened in the village; there was nothing to do. Morning was light, night was light. I kneeled upon the sand and watched the icebergs come and go, collapsing, capsizing, and causing sudden surf—watched them glisten in warm sunlight and rain down turquoise tears.

Hans's daughter Marie Louisa, then six years old, became my special friend. Every morning she practiced English and I Greenlandic; then our day of exploring began. We walked to and fro in the mountains, up and down the beach. She liked to take off her clothes and go for quick dips in the Arctic sea; then we'd clamber up the amphitheater of brown rock behind the village, collecting rocks and tiny alpine flowers, and bathe in a waterfall, since no one in the village has bathtubs or showers. She slept beside me on the floor and called me *Anana*—Mother—and when it was time for me to leave at the end of the summer, I felt the green melancholy of life in the lower latitudes creep in and felt sure we would always, somehow, be joined.

When I started out traveling to Greenland in 1993, I was still quite fragile from an accident two years earlier: I had been hit by lightning while taking a walk on my ranch in Wyoming. As I felt stronger each year, my parents, who had saved my life by coming for me in Wyoming and bringing me to a cardiologist who plucked me from death's dizzying grasp, had begun slowing down. My father was ill and my mother was going blind. Her failing eyesight was the weld that bound me to the long, all-dark, all-light seasons in Greenland—I learned about seeing in the dark, about going blind in the sunlight. Though my obligation to my parents forced me to return often to California to care for them, Greenland was a siren singing me back and I began climbing the latitudinal ladder of Greenland's massive west coast.

The next spring I flew to Avanersuaq—the far north, to Rasmussen's Greenland, to live and travel with what he called "the Polar Eskimos." Up there subsistence hunting goes on year-round, by dogsled on the sea ice in winter and spring and by kayak in the short summer months of open water. April, May, and June is *uutooq*—hunting for seals, and for walrus and narwhal at the ice edge. Fall is the best time for walrus hunting, when the new ice has just come in—usually by October—and

July and August is the time for hunting narwhal with harpoons from a kayak.

In May 1996, I arrived in Qaanaaq to go out with Jens Danielson, an Inuit hunter in his late 30s who had followed Knud Rasmussen's tracks and traveled by dogsled all the way across the polar north, from Greenland to Point Hope, Alaska. Jens is a big man of great modesty and reserve. The night I met him and Niels, his friend who would translate for me, I wondered if I was doing the right thing—going off alone on the ice with two strange men. That night, in bright sun and cool air, the dogs began howling. Greenland's silence is such that the dog-songs seem to travel everywhere: up the rocky cliffs to the ice cap, across the frozen ocean to Ellesmere Island, in and out of the villages.

Thule-style sleds are big—14 feet long—and are pulled by 15 or 20 dogs in a fan-hitch, so they can travel under the trace-lines and visit each other while pulling. I couldn't sleep. The next morning, I met Niels and Jens with my duffel bag. The ice was crowded with a thousand dogs, sleds, children playing, hunters packing to go out for a month. Jens piled our gear on the sled, laid caribou skins on top, and lashed everything down with rope. Then he hitched up the dogs and we were off, careering over rough ice, following the coast north to Siorapaluk, the northernmost village in the world, and beyond, going wherever there were seals.

The dogsled was a platform for viewing the world and letting the weather inside and the weather without mingle. Storms burst into being on the horizon ahead of us, marched into us, traveled through our bodies as we traveled in the midst of its snowy flesh, and when they ended, the silence taught us to listen with an accurate ear. The panting of 20 dogs pulling hard was the contrapuntal beat to which our thoughts were tapped out, and when the dogs stopped to rest, all thinking stopped. I learned then the Greenlandic word that is central to their culture: *sila*, which means both weather and consciousness.

For subsistence hunters, inside and outside, internal and external, are one and the same. The keenness of mind that allows the hunter to find food for himself, his dogs, and family every day in the harshest climate in the world is etched into his synapses by weather. Conversely, consciousness exists everywhere and in everything. The Inuit know that animals understand everything we do and that we can understand them. Once, we all spoke the same language. What outsiders routinely describe as the Arctic's desolate waste is really a hospitable place full of animals and spirits, voices and stories. The four months of sunlight and the four of darkness is a kind of generosity in which the imagination and the weather can become unanchored. By comparison, our continual and repetitive alteration of day and night is bewildering.

Jens, Niels, and I went here and there in Jens's "neighborhood" of ice. What looked like an exotic coastline to others was only his backyard. Fog bent mountainsides and glaciers; snow slowed the dogs to a walk. Jens said that one spring it snowed so much he had to load the dogs on the sled and pull it himself. Continual light became our friend. Our circadian rhythms looped and gallivanted. Who cared about time? We started off in the afternoon, arrived somewhere at one in the morning, ate dinner at 3 a.m., slept until who knows when, then harnessed the dogs and began moving again. Some days there was nothing to hunt and we went hungry except for the Danish cookies and bread we'd brought along from the *butik* in the village. Other times there was plenty of seal to eat—Jens boiled it—and, per Eskimo fashion, we ate and ate, sometimes for three hours, until it was all gone.

Greenland hunters wear skins—from the animals they eat. "We eat the inside and wear the outside," they like to say. In the cold times we wore polar bear pants, arctic hare socks, sealskin *kamiks* (boots) rubbed with polar bear grease to keep them waterproof, sealskin mittens with dog-hair ruffs, and fox-fur anoraks. In the old days, men and women wore eider duck underwear, but no one makes it anymore. Farther south, where it is warmer, the hunters wear sealskin pants and anoraks. Lying on our sleds, we looked like seals traveling over seals, ingesting them to become like them.

Inside all those exquisite spring days of light, the memory of darkness and of hunger is never far away. The ethnographic notes of Knud Rasmussen are full of tales of starvation, hunger, accidents, bad weather, and cannibalism. Jens reminded me of the time when one winter merged into another and there was nothing to hunt because the ice was closed. Such times can always come, and storms and bad ice can always take you away. That is why we like to be always moving. So that we can choose the life and the death we are having. We don't know anything about tomorrow or yesterday. Just now. That's what we know, and that seal up there, who will maybe let me shoot and eat him…. *Imaqa*. Maybe. Nothing more.

Later that year, when the sun went down for good after the briefest of summers—when purple saxifrage blooms and goes to seed in three weeks and a caterpillar can take 14 years to become a butterfly, freezing solid each winter, then thawing out again to continue its slow progression—then the new ice began to come in like great windowpanes, translucent and watery, and Jens said how difficult it was to tell the difference between water and new ice, and that only by knowing the difference could you survive. Then the darkness came, and the ice under us became the source of light, a kind of subterranean moon, which alone would teach us the difference between water and ice, how to see, and why to keep moving.

Matsang Tsangpo Valley, Nyalam County, Tibet ED DOUGLAS

the church of my choice ✳ ED DOUGLAS

A man's work is nothing but this slow trek to rediscover,
through the detours of art, those two or three great and simple images
in whose presence his heart first opened.

ALBERT CAMUS

TIBET, ON THE EAST SIDE OF EVEREST. Standing in the tent doorway, I watched the snow falling thickly. Behind me, Kalsang poured hot water into an aluminum bowl at my feet. The cloud had sunk more firmly onto the low hills surrounding a nearby lake and pasture; the mountains themselves were half forgotten. Crouching at the bowl, I took some soap and slowly washed my hands as the snow settled thickly on my sweater and in my hair. Stray flakes slipped between my collar and my neck, melting against my spine. Scooping water in my hands, I splashed my face and beard before taking the towel, filthy and damp, from the tent's door tie. Kalsang took the bowl away, and he handed me a cup of tea. I lit a cigarette and exhaled.

"Where's Norbu?"

Kalsang straightened and paused, lips compressed, eyes narrowing against the snow and mist. He looked into the foggy distance and shook his head. Then we heard singing. Behind us, toward the lake, yaks were moving slowly across the pasture, bells clanking each time they bent their shaggy heads to tear at the grass still visible through the thickening snow. Norbu was wheeling between them, arms outstretched, skipping his feet round at each revolution. His strong, penetrating voice cut through the dank evening, hard edged in the soft air, seeming closer than the 80 yards that separated us. It was an old song, resigned but not sorrowful, catching space and distance in its music. The dancing suited the weather, not the mood. He saw us watching and stopped, hand covering mouth as he laughed in embarrassment.

"He likes to dance," Kalsang said, ducking back inside the tent to make dinner.

Norbu wandered over, and when he saw I was smoking, he put two fingers to his lips, puffing and grinning widely. He made to stamp on my feet and then grabbed my sleeve and put out his hand. I shook my head in refusal. Norbu and I had three things in common. We both liked beer, we both smoked, and we'd both lost our fathers the year before. Norbu, being 11 years old, had more justification in feeling cheated by this.

"What happened?" I had asked Kalsang one evening. He spoke quickly to Norbu in Tibetan without looking up from the *dahl*. Norbu replied just as quickly and looked away.

"He got sick," Kalsang told me. I could have let it drop, but the reasons for fathers dying were at the front of my mind.

"How did he get sick? What kind of sickness?" There was another brief exchange. Norbu lifted his chin as he spoke, defiant, even angry.

"Lungs. Coughing. A bad cough." He did not elaborate. As Kalsang stirred the soup, Norbu looked out of the tent. I guessed pneumonia. After meeting Norbu's mother, I decided that the father must have been in his early 40s. Death doesn't wait for the invitation of old age in rural Tibet; it just turns up unannounced.

Kalsang pressed another cup of tea into my hands, and I watched Norbu getting ready for bed with the other yak herders, Tashi and N'wang. They had made a nest from the rugs normally thrown over the yaks to protect their hides from the straps and wooden saddles. The three of them would curl up together for warmth under a pile of more blankets. We were at 16,500 feet, and with darkness fallen, the temperature had dropped still further below freezing. N'wang was 15 or 16 and in charge of the yaks. He wore a thick sweater tucked inside his cheap cotton pants hitched up with a black plastic belt so that several inches of ankle were exposed. He walked at a steady pace throughout the day while Norbu rushed and whirled around him, chasing stray beasts and dancing as he went.

Norbu pulled off his battered green Chinese pumps, and his socks steamed with condensation. They hadn't been dry for a week. Off came his heavy woolen pants with the turned-up cuffs, revealing stick legs and bright red long johns. He caught me watching him again, and we grinned at each other. He rubbed his arms and blew hard, rolling his eyes at the cold. All of these young herders were ill. Tashi had weeping sores on his face. Norbu and N'wang would cough and hack through the night. Wriggling into my thick down sleeping bag at the other end of the tent, it was I who seemed the child.

✳

NEXT MORNING the clouds and mist had rolled back a little, and the east side of Chomo-lungma towered above us. People in Kharta translate the name as "big fat hen" and, staring across at the coxcomb of pinnacles on its northeast ridge, I could see why. But I'm sure there's a story behind the naming too. I had learned that there are always stories. Every lake, every pass, every feature or cave in the cliffs, every tree, every bird carries its own story.

"Look at the trees," Kalsang had told me as we walked into the Kama Valley, above the pastures at Tsok-sham. I lifted my face to the crowns of the biggest junipers I'd ever seen. The wind had bent the upper section of the trunks in a northeasterly direction. "They are holy trees," Kalsang said. "They are facing Sakya, saying prayers." The thousand-year-old monastery at Sakya had been the political center of Tibet in the 13th century, and this region had come under its control. The lamas allied themselves with the Mongols to save their faith and their way of life. As the Mongols faded from history, so too did the influence of Sakya within Tibet. Later, the Nyingmapa and then the Gelupka took control, here as well as in Lhasa. Politics, religion, which way the wind blows, all caught in the shape of a juniper tree.

Such beliefs permeate the people. In a village in Kharta, I had shown a farmer a picture of his home taken a dozen years before with a group of people sitting outside it. The farmer ran his thick finger across the faces.

"That's me," he said. "That's my father."

"Where is he now?"

"He's dead. He died a long time ago."

"He doesn't look old in that photo."

"He was maybe 40."

"What happened? Was he sick?"

"He cut down a tree."

"How did that kill him?"

"'It was the wrong tree. It was a holy tree. After that he got sick."

In the West, we believe that pathogens infect your blood and overwhelm your immune system. Trees do not have spirits. We project these explanations onto the landscape around us to comfort ourselves that there are reasons and purposes in which we can trust, that there are narratives that we can control. In this belief system, my father was a big man with a damaged heart. Nobody cut down the wrong tree.

❋

In the pastures northeast of Tsok-sham, the nomad Jung-mo was preparing to return with her yaks over the Shao La for the winter. She has made this journey once a year for all her life, and her parents before her, escaping the mountains before the snows close the pass. Her sons were with her, but her second husband had been dead for many years. Her first husband is now a monk in India, and she hadn't seen their only child, a daughter, for 40 years. Father and daughter had fled the Chinese in 1959. To go to Dharmsala, where her daughter is working, she said, means a trip to Lhasa to get her papers in order. "They won't give me papers anyway," she said, wiping her greasy hands on her apron. So she stays, walking the paths, thinking of what has gone. Her life blends continuity with fracture.

Behind her in the small tent, Jung-mo's eldest boy churned butter into the tea. The smoke was choking, and I sprawled with my face near the floor to catch the sweet air that filtered through the door. Rain drummed against the tent fabric, woven from yak hair, but only the flat gray afternoon light seeped through. Behind the fireplace was a small altar with a photograph of the Dalai Lama at its center. When Jung-mo heard that we were planning to cross the Langma La to the north, she told us of a lake we should visit.

"It's near Tso-sho-rimi," she said, referring to a better-known lake that appears on maps as Shurim-tso. "If you're a good person, then you can see the future in its water. It's called Tso-me-lung. You should go there. Now, have some more tea."

Several days later, below the Langma La, I looked back at the broad spread of grassland that hangs above the Kama River, wondering which lake she had meant. Each one has its own legend. I could sense the matrix of stories linking one place to the next and the paths between. In the snow at my feet I found a group of gentian blooms, their petals frozen solid. Snowcocks scattered across the crags above my head as the yaks drew closer to where I had stopped. Kalsang and I reached the pass together. He showed me striations in the rock where spirits had been turned to stone and pointed to where rocks had fallen from the ridge to leave a near circular hole. "Many years ago," Kalsang said, "a lama came and opened a window in the mountain to see if the people in Kharta were ready for Buddhism. And they were, so he went down into the valley."

I would watch Kalsang intently when he told me these stories. I wanted to know how much he believed them to be true and how much to be myth. And I knew that the question would never occur to him. The truth lies in the telling of the stories, not in the stories themselves. We have thrived, do thrive on this. We have covered the face of the Earth telling our stories.

In the time of the gods, Wangpo Gyajin offered 500 lotus flowers to Avalokitesvara, the bodhisattva of Compassion and Tibet's patron deity. One fell from the sky, coming to Earth in the heart of the Himalaya, where Tibet and India meet. This lotus became the hidden sacred valley of Beyul Khembalung, full of aromatic and medicinal flowers and, like the other *beyul* in Tibet, a place of refuge for Buddhists from war and calamity. The valley's origin was revealed by the Indian master Guru Rinpoche to Trisong Detsen, Tibet's greatest king. It was opened, unlocked in a spiritual sense, by Rigdzin Godem, who thus earned the title of *tertön*, or discoverer. All this is recorded in Beyul Khembalung's *neyig*— the region's spiritual guide-text. Was this the story Kalsang was telling, half-lost, half-forgotten? Was Rigdzin Godem the one who opened the window from Langma La, the beyul's inner gate, and looked into the Kama Valley?

"There," Kalsang told me as we walked below the Langma La, pointing to a cave at the head of the Rabkar glacier, "that is where Guru Rinpoche meditated. And Milarepa too."

Until the political chaos of the 1960s, mystics, celebrated tantrists, women and men, continued to live in isolation in these remote valleys. In the cave above the turquoise lake of Tshechu, is the monastery of Gang La, called Namdag Lhe Phodang, "god's pure palace." Here the world was left behind, its distractions and excess, in a pure relationship with the land and the ideas that reside within the land, the bones of our story. ("There is no concurrence of bone," T.S. Eliot wrote of Glencoe, another place distinguished by sorrow.) These are the patterns of all our lives. Despite the ruin and loss of the past 40 years, prompted by the Chinese occupation, nomads and farmers still make pilgrimage to the beyul's holy places, the latter most often in August, before they are busy with the harvest, when the monsoon cloaks the mountains and the flowers flood the valley with color and fragrance, especially the blue poppy, Its local name, *upa medog*, recalls the blue lotus that fell to Earth and formed this valley of peace.

The second version of this land's story is not myth, or at least, closer to truth. But it seems less real, less in keeping with our expectations, our preconceptions about this place because stories compete for our attention. On a clear day from the narrow, rocky defile of the Shao La, the pass Jung-mo would cross soon with her yaks, you can see the gigantic pyramid of Makalu. Stretching across the pass, from one steep ridge across the flat dip of the saddle and up the ridge on its opposite side, is a high dry-stone wall. Why was it built? To keep the gods in and the demons out? To protect some metaphysical ideal from pollution? None and all of this. The wall was built in the late 18th century to keep out the marauding armies of the great Gorkhali king Prithvi Narayan Shah, who, when he captured the city of Kirtipur, not far from Kathmandu, cut off the noses of almost a thousand of his adversaries, a punishment usually reserved for adulterous women, filling several baskets with 80 pounds of bloody remains. Not a man to be taken lightly.

It is hardly surprising that Tibet's army, despite hastily built fortifications whose remains can still be seen on the plains around Dingri, didn't stand much of a chance—even though by the time the Gorkhalis arrived, their fearsome king was dead. Tibet had been warlike once, but pride and courage don't automatically translate into military skill, and anyway, they'd lost the knack. The war with Nepal left deep scars on the people and the land. When Charles Howard-Bury led the first expedition to Everest in 1921, over 130 years later, population numbers had still not recovered and the ruins of villages and forts were all around. The Nepalis had reached Shigatse before the Chinese intervened and drove them out, sending an army across the Himalaya deep into Nepal. They built a fort on the hill above Dingri—its remains are still visible—and there was a Chinese garrison there for many years afterward. Howard-Bury found their books and papers hastily thrown away when the Tibetans finally got rid of them; he lodged his expedition in an abandoned Chinese guest house that the Tibetans would not go near because of the ghosts that surrounded it. They were still terrified of the Gorkhalis and were paying 5,000 rupees a month in tribute. Howard-Bury saw these things, although not the beyul itself, nor the stories nor the paths between the stories. But he saw the flowers and the beasts, understood the warp and weft of legend and reality. George Mallory, on the other hand, walked straight past it all, intent on building his own narrative among the white peaks.

And the story now is the same story again. The shopkeeper has a fine house a few hundred yards from the compound at Kharta. But the land here is harsh, drier and colder than the valley a few miles to the southwest. The soil is hard, difficult to plow, and the afternoon wind howls across the plain, forcing his family to shelter behind their walls where juniper is stacked in anticipation of the winter. Despite these deprivations, the shopkeeper seems a happy man. He has a 30-inch television on which his mother-in-law, 80 if she's a day, is watching a Jackie Chan movie through thick spectacles. The shopkeeper has provided well for his daughter; there are new blankets for winter and plenty to eat. He smiles and says little, but this is what his smile says: "There are medicines and schools for the children. And all this for a little give-and-take with the Chinese in Tashidzom. What have we lost? Nothing. It doesn't stop us praying. It's true that there are only a few lamas now and those that remain are old, but there were too many of them in the old days and my family had to work even harder for them. Now I have land, my own land. The Chinese build roads, hospitals. Why shouldn't we welcome them? It's progress. Why can't we have the things you have? A place of peace? A place of stagnation, more like. All those hermits meditating in their freezing caves—what good did any of that do us?"

✳

WHAT ARE THESE LANDSCAPES FOR? These wild places where people survive rather than dominate, here on the margins where land is too poor to farm for anything but subsistence, too remote from the great cities of the world to be of any account at all. For explorers it's a blank slate on which they can scratch their names. I came here first, they say. I marked this land first; my story was the first story. Except it's rarely true, and so often those people who have been here all along have had their stories reduced to the status of academic footnotes. Yet that isn't the way most of us feel. We aren't interested in all that exploring stuff, at least not for ourselves. We're in it for the freedom nature offers us. To be surrounded by living things, to feel part of life's patterns, that's enough. The biologist E.O. Wilson wrote:

"We are human in good part because of the particular way we affiliate with other organisms. They are the matrix in which the human mind originated and is permanently rooted, and they offer the challenge and freedom innately sought. To the extent that each person can feel like a naturalist, the old excitement of the untrammeled world will be regained."

We have a relationship with nature, we invest in its indifference the stories of our lives, the hardships and the promises of what the future may hold. We plant our crops and lay our dead to rest in it. Mother and daughter, father and son, we weave our individual selves together by the stories we tell. Without this we are naked and without hope. We leave these marks on the land in countless ways, the marks of our passing, forming a thread that we cannot choose to abandon, the nature inside us.

✴

CLIMBING DOWN TO THE RIVER IS AWKWARD. The stones are coated in moss and are damp from the heavy rain that's been falling all morning. Finally I'm standing on a flat ledge above a weir, the water curving in a white, frothing arc. This river has been bent to serve industry, although not broken. Around me are tall factories and warehouses, some of them still in use, some derelict, some converted into apartments, their brick and sandstone walls scrubbed new. The landscape of northern England is once more in the agonies of evolution. Across the river is a tangle of thick scrub, birch trees, and patches of fern wreathed around old car tires and an abandoned easy chair. Scraps of plastic snag on rocks, cans rust, cardboard rots. A pair of wagtails skim across the water, and from the bridge upstream comes the dull roar of traffic.

In my hand is a brown metal urn. Crouching by the rushing water, I carefully ease off its lid, open the plastic bag inside and sprinkle some of the ashes in my palm. These are all the physical remains of my father. For a moment I can see him sitting at home on the sofa, legs stretched out, another long day at the office behind him, in a life of long days. And me still young enough to sit down next to him, under his outstretched arm, and rest my head on his thick chest and listen to the slow, even beat of his heart, as solid as the rocks studding the riverbed below me. I can see him sitting in the kitchen reading, looking up and greeting me in a voice deep and warm that I hear now only when I sleep. I turn to look behind me. Standing on the embankment above me are my mother and three sisters. They are all crying. We're an emotional family and, for all his faults—quickness of temper, a stiletto sense of the put-down—my father was a good man who felt things deeply and loved deeply too. Something in each of us, in the core of each of us, has been ripped away, leaving only the shape of itself to confirm our loss. He did a passable imitation of Sinatra, thought Jimmy Stewart was how actors were supposed to be, had fought in a war, and enjoyed an inexplicable affinity for tasteless baseball caps.

He was also a steelworker. Or, at least, that is how he described himself on his marriage certificate. And it was true; he was a steelworker, inasmuch as he worked at running a steel-works. For several years he ran the biggest stainless steel plant in Europe. I can remember acutely the sensation of walking into its vast space, hearing the ponderous rumble of gigantic machinery, the crash of tons of scrap being fed into the crucible, the acrid fumes scraping my throat. The white flash of molten steel made the darkness above even deeper, the sky just a memory. In pools of weak electric light, workers moved with purpose, competent and assured. This was industry; this was the business of great nations.

As a child, I had no concept of the burden this immense enterprise placed on my father. This was the period when the British steel industry was being dismantled. In South Yorkshire, where we lived and he worked, more than 50,000 men and women lost their jobs in a quarter of a century. Mile after mile of derelict factories and steelworks rotted in the winter rain. Sheffield sank into poverty and recrimination, its stories, its sense of self, diminished.

Things got better, slowly. Whenever some unthinking metropolitan sophisticate exposed his patronizing underbelly with comments on Sheffield's demise, the old man would take pleasure in pointing out that the city—at that moment, his city— was making more steel than it had in World War II with a tenth of the workforce. As a youth I found liberty on the purple moors and rough crags that rise above the city; he found solidarity among the heroes of its industrial age. "I wanted to make things that were useful," he told me when I asked him why this path and not another.

A long legacy lay behind him. Sheffield made the tools and steel for Victorian Britain, its railways and ships, its guns and machinery. And, for much of the 19th century, for America too. It rose almost as quickly as the works closed a century and a half later. When Spear & Jackson built its tool factory in Sheffield's East End during the mid-19th century, the site was farmland. Within decades the landscape had been overwhelmed, fields and trees cleared for furnaces, and workers' houses built as far as the eye could see. It was a new world; human history had seen nothing like this. In *A Picturesque History of Yorkshire*, published in the 1880s, J.S. Fletcher drew a grim impression of the city:

"Under smoke and rain, Sheffield is suggestive of nothing so much as of the popular conception of the infernal regions. From the chimneys, great volumes of smoke pour their listless way towards a forbidding sky; out of the furnaces shoot forth great tongues of flame which relieve the somberness of the scene and illuminate it at the same time; in the streets there is a substratum of dust and mud; in the atmosphere a choking something that appears to take a firm grip of one's throat. The aspect of the northern fringe of Sheffield on such a day is terrifying, the black heaps of refuse, the rows of cheerless-looking houses, the thousand and one signs of grinding industrial life, the inky waters of river and canal, the general darkness and dirt of the whole scene serves but to create feelings of repugnance and even horror."

I fell in with this line pretty early on, even though Sheffield was an utterly different place when we went to live there. You could drink the water and breathe the air, for a start. Children weren't poisoned by the filth, there were theaters and galleries, football clubs and working-men's clubs, societies and fellowships. But it all seemed so dull to me. England was an uncertain place in those years; even punk had lost its edge. And like many adolescents, I transformed a sneering attitude into an intelligent ethos: "Industry, bad; wide open spaces, good. And romantic." My father was very patient with this, as he often was with the big things. "When are you going to give up the climbing?" he asked me once, pulling up outside the house one rainy afternoon. "I wasn't planning to," I told him. It wasn't mentioned again. If he was disappointed, he never said. But then again, he got me in the end. Maybe he knew he would.

He knew the landscape of Sheffield better than I. There is no better evidence of this than the shocking discovery I made. Along the bank of the River Don, I found a colony of fig trees. They shouldn't have been there. Luxuriant, exotic, and so not a part of an industrial northern town's props list. When I told my father, he rolled his eyes and threw up his hands in mock disgust. He knew all about them. The river, he told me, flanked by the belching furnaces and molten steel, was used to quench the hot metal, and as a consequence, its temperature rose to a mean of around 20°C, plenty warm enough for the germination of fig seeds tossed into the water by, the legend tells, steelworkers eating their lunch. All the trees are 70 years old, because after that period changes in steelmaking took the pressure off the weary, overheated Don and the water cooled. New seeds went ungerminated. No new trees grew. Steelmen knew the story, others did not. One day the bosses at a chain of pubs determined to dig up the fig tree outside one of their Sheffield houses down by the river. The locals told them to keep it just where it was. Because it was the wrong tree. It was a holy tree.

✳

DRIVING LATE ONE NIGHT across the Peak District, heavy with sleep, I catch a glimpse of powerful lights flickering across the sky. Lightning, I think to myself, and carry on. But the lights are across the whole sky, swelling and fading in a way lightning just doesn't. I pull over and get out of the car, feeling the wind cutting sharply though my light clothes. Shivering, exhausted, I stand mesmerized as the northern lights spread across the black night, wrapped in the mystery of it all. What would those who went before have thought of it? There would have been a story, because there always is, of good crops or the end of the world, of pestilence or the birth of a child.

Around me the moors stretched out. These were the places I went as a child. Then I thought it was wildness I was pursuing— the absence of factories, shops, the prosaic suburbs. The heather and bracken stretched purple in summer, gold in the autumn, uninterrupted by the politics of fences, the greed of construction. I was free of that. But, of course, the moors were a consequence of agriculture, the scrub cleared and kept down. The land was scarred with ancient quarries and mines, the caves spread with debris from the Stone Age. Ground elder that I thought wild had been planted by medieval monks, the eddies in the river improved to let trout breed. The land was worked and molded just like the River Don in the heart of the city. My climbing was just a small part of all those older stories, examining the rock for weakness, feeling its shape and what it can tolerate with the same assurance as men once shaped tools from stone. The wilderness, the idea of wilderness, was just another way of looking at things. The story of the fig trees taught me that.

All of us have spent our weekends walking on paths, by ourselves or with our children. Before cars and trains, before industry, before iron, before art, we walked the same trails, generation after generation. In the Peak, the oldest paths take you to scrapes in the ground, half-collapsed barrows, empty graves, sometimes set on ridges where they can be seen from miles around, often on the fringes of ancient pasture. The living next to the dead. Archaeologists investigating these prehistorical burial grounds have found all kinds of bones. They have concluded that the inhabitants of this old world would handle them, mark them, dismantle skeletons, even place them in new graves. Shamans would use the remains in ritual, crawl into barrows to sleep with the dead and dream visions of the future. In this way the stories of those gone before intermingled with those of the present and those who would follow. The stories of the past were maintained, developed, to match changes in their lives and the landscape they relied upon. The ancients were making sense of things, of loss and change, and of themselves, telling stories about why things are. On the banks of the River Don, I open my hand and spread my father's ashes onto the water. They float on the surface for a moment and then are gone, absorbed by the current, swept away downstream by the endless flow.

Proposed trellis, Adam Joseph Lewis Center, Oberlin College BARNEY TAXEL

a new geography of hope ✳ WILLIAM MCDONOUGH
MICHAEL BRAUNGART

Landscape, Design, and the Renewal
of Ecological Intelligence

IMAGINE SEEKING REVELATIONS on the weedy edge of a Kmart parking lot. It may sound absurd on the face of it, but there is a long tradition of meditating on landscapes extremely antagonistic to life in order to understand life itself. In the biblical tradition, the pilgrimage to the desert wilderness is seen as a journey to a barren, forbidding place that nonetheless offers a vision of renewal. "Going to the mountain" has become parlance for having something serious to think about. The inhospitable places of the contemporary world—brownfields, landfills, abandoned neighborhoods—are the work of human hands, but they too are natural landscapes with a revelatory power all their own. The

expanse of asphalt surrounding a strip mall may express ignorance of the living Earth, but it is nonetheless a shaping of land
by earthly creatures. Like a beaver dam or an anthill, it is rich
with information and metaphor about the relation between the
laws of nature and the design of the world we inhabit. A lot of
this information may be negative feedback—the asphalt heating
up in the noonday sun, for example—but to ignore the signals of
human presence is to miss an opportunity to engage the extremities of the landscapes we have created and, by design, to lay the
foundation for their renewal.

Seeing hope in the extremities of the human world begins
with our perception of landscape. For North Americans the landscapes most often associated with renewal are the iconic images
of the sublime and distant wilderness. Wallace Stegner captured
this sense of the wild in his "Wilderness Letter" of 1960. When
Stegner wrote his famous plea for wild country, the daily lives of
most Americans were so remote from the landscapes of mountain, forest, and tallgrass prairie, he was obliged to appeal for the
preservation of the idea of wilderness. If the wild was no longer
the landscape against which we took our measure, or even a place
we knew, he wrote, "the reminder and the reassurance that it is
still there is good for our spiritual health even if we never once
in ten years set foot in it."

"We simply need that wild country available to us," he continued, "even if we never do more than drive to its edge and look
in. For it can be a means of reassuring ourselves of our sanity as
creatures, a part of the geography of hope."

He was right, of course. Wild places are sacred, and even
infrequent pilgrimages to see them can inspire a sense of wonder
and a reverence for life. But perhaps we have taken Stegner too

literally. Perhaps a distant wilderness, an idea of wild country, positions nature too far from our daily lives. Stegner himself was intimate with his surroundings yet North Americans tend to think that true nature can only be found on the pristine, remote extremities of civilization and that these places have little to do with the everyday human world. Culture is here, nature far away. The trouble is not the idea of protecting and preserving wilderness. It's that the design of the world we inhabit—our communities, our workplaces, our economy—is so impermeable to nature, it is all too easy to leave our reverence in the parking lots of national parks.

This separation from natural landscapes, our sense of looking in from the edge, is reinforced by the picturesque, the sense of the land as a static backdrop. But landscape has more lively meanings, too. Tracing the word's deeper roots, the landscape architect Anne Whiston Spirn finds meanings that suggest that landscape is in every sense our home. In Danish, German, and Old English, she writes, "landscape associates people and place." *Land* "means both a place and the people living there," and the roots of *-scape* suggest an active, sensual, aesthetic partnership with other life.

Indeed, writes Spirn, "all living things share the same space, all make landscape." For humans, to dwell in a place, to cultivate soil or build a town, is to be a "co-author" of landscape with trees, wind, water, plants, and animals. A deep knowledge of the dynamics of these connections—the language of landscape—can create fluent dialogues with place. Absent contact with the natural world, however, the language of landscape is easily forgotten.

We live in a time when our dialogues with place are not very fluent. The discordant strains, some subtle, some ghastly, are written on the landscape. They may be unnoticeable, without a sense of history, as in the enclosing of the central lawn of the University of Virginia in 1890, which compromised the openness of Thomas Jefferson's design and obscured the school's relationship to the surrounding countryside and the nearby Blue Ridge Mountains. In Jefferson's original plan, notes Spirn, the open lawn "linked two sources of knowledge: books and nature." Notes of discord may also be produced by an absence, as on the naked streets of cities where to plant a tree or to garden is to enter a Byzantine world of regulations designed to keep nature at bay. These are the more subtle expressions of dissonance. Others scream. There are, for example, the extremities of the worlds we protect and those we burden with waste: the majesty of Rocky Mountain National Park and Yucca Mountain, the proposed site of a future nuclear waste dump on sacred Shoshone land; the astonishing heights of Denali and the equally astonishing Fresh Kills, the 2,000-acre landfill on the marshlands of Staten Island, a mountain of trash so big it is the highest point on the eastern seaboard. And sometimes these landscapes are one, as on the hallowed slopes of Mount Everest, where sherpas last year hauled out from a high-elevation Base Camp more than four tons of discarded oxygen bottles, garbage, and human waste.

None of us need look too far to see some element of these extremities; contemporary architecture recapitulates them in the built environment. Designers, architects, landscape architects, and engineers, after all, mediate the boundary between people and nature. Working with mass, membrane, and transparency, the designs of buildings and grounds are either responsive to place—which tends to engage people and materials in dialogues with the natural world—or exist in stark isolation from their surroundings.

The latter is the industrial norm. Many architects today, for example, no longer rely on the sun to heat or illuminate buildings, and consequently few know how to find true south, let alone converse with landscape. And so we find in our homes, cities, and workplaces the disconnection between culture and nature.

At its most extreme, this disconnection yields artifacts like Biosphere 2, a landscape co-authored not with the surrounding Sonoran Desert, but with a dream of outer space, a fantasy marriage between the worlds of EPCOT (Experimental Prototypical Community of Tomorrow) and ecology. Conceived to test the feasibility of a self-sustaining space colony, the glass-and-aluminum domes of the three-acre Biosphere 2 were built to re-create the Earth's natural systems in a completely sealed-off, human-made world. As reported in the *New York Times*, "the aim was to have human inhabitants thrive in a miniature world made of sea, savanna, mangrove swamp, rain forest, desert and farm, the areas and atmospheres interacting to form a totally independent life-support system."

In September 1991, the first crew of eight Biospherians was sealed inside the structure; as their first year drew to a close, recalled the *Times* report, things began to go awry. Air temperatures soared. Oxygen and carbon dioxide levels fluctuated wildly. Brittle tree limbs collapsed and desert became chaparral. All the pollinators died, as did 19 of 25 vertebrate species. The only insects to survive were katydids, cockroaches, and an exotic species of ant known as *Paratrechina longicornus*—the crazy ant—which swarmed over every ecosystem in the enclosure. During the second year of the crew's stay, the complex needed to be regularly resuscitated with oxygen, and by 1994 attempts at self-sufficient living were abandoned. Despite annual energy inputs costing up to $1 million, the regulation of biogeochemical cycles in a closed ecosystem proved to be more complex than imagined.

While the designers of Biosphere 2 hoped to create a hermetically sealed building—that was the purpose of their experiment—we can find this an instructive cautionary tale. In some imaginations the fantasy of Biosphere 2 suggests that we are actually capable of reinventing and controlling the natural systems that have evolved over billions of years to create life on Earth. Such a view treats us as little more than machines, which need only regulated nutrient flows to survive, but don't need an unobstructed view of the sky, or the feel of a natural breeze on the skin, or the taste of fresh fruit from a nearby tree rooted in the deep, inimitable microcosmos of the Earth's soil.

This is not to gainsay technology or scientific inquiry; both are crucial to the human prospect. But in these technologically marvelous times we would do well to consider what we intend with our technical innovations. The unexamined innovations of the industrial revolution gave us a civilization that uses technology to overcome the rules of the natural world, and, along with astonishing wealth, we got a century of extraordinary ecological decline. Indeed, the enthusiasts of space colonies need only travel to the copper mines of Chile or the nickel mines of Ontario to find a landscape devoid of earthly life. Sadly, we don't need to go so far to see the world's unraveling.

Barren landscapes, however, are not the inevitable outcome of the human presence in the world. They are instead the result of design failures that express just how little we know of our place on Earth. But design can also express ecological intelligence, which is rooted in the intention to understand the nature of interdependence rather than the application of brute force.

Attuned to the flow of natural processes, ecologically intelligent design, we could say, is the practice of the language of landscape, the performance of fluent dialogues with place. An ecologically intelligent designer, rather than shutting the world out, attends to the way nature works, seeking information from the unique characteristics of locale. The availability of sunlight, shade, and water; the subtleties of climate and terrain; the health of local birds, flowers, and grasses all become fundamental to design. And when the making of a broad spectrum of things—from buildings and energy systems to cities and regional plans—is informed by a mindfulness to the particularities of place, we might begin to experience nature's reemergence in our everyday lives and see the landscape anew.

Exploring the use of mass, membrane, and transparency in architecture reveals how design can participate in landscape. Biosphere 2 is an extreme example of an impermeable membrane, but it is really only the logical extension of the controlled environment of a Phoenix high-rise, which uses glass to create the illusion of transparency. The windows provide distant views but don't open; people are trapped indoors while the heat of the sun pours in and air conditioning creates a habitable interior world. But there is a signal of a new design strategy in another way of living in the desert, practiced by a culture that has perfected the art of permeability—the Bedouin.

Bedu is the Arabic word for "inhabitant of the desert." For centuries the Bedouin tribes migrated from oasis to oasis in the deserts of Arabia and the Sinai. They moved about in a land in which every element of survival—food, water, soil, energy—was devastatingly rare. And yet the culture that emerged from these extremities could hardly be called arid. Instead, from a deep understanding of the harsh realities of the land grew both a fierce protectiveness of territory and a rich tradition of music, poetry, hospitality, and elegant design.

The Bedouin tent, for example, shows how simple and elegant—how suited to locale—good design can be. On the move in their migratory rounds, the Bedouin needed shelter that was both portable and reliable in a variety of conditions. On the plains of the Sinai, temperatures often rise above 120°F. There is neither shade nor breeze. But the black Bedouin tent of coarsely woven goat hair provides a breathing membrane. The black surface creates a deep shade while the coarse weave diffuses the sunlight, creating a beautifully illuminated interior. As the sun heats the dark fabric, hot air rises above the tent and air from inside is drawn out, in effect creating a cooling breeze. When it rains—as even in the desert it sometimes does—the woven fibers swell, the tiny holes in the fabric close, and the structure becomes tight. The tent is lightweight and portable and can be easily repaired; the fabric factory—the goats— followed the Bedouin around, providing valuable wool while transforming the botany of the desert into horn, skins, meat, milk, butter, and cheese. When the tent wears out, it can be composted, returning nutrients to the precious soil of a river valley oasis. This ingenious design, locally relevant and culturally rich, makes the desert skyscraper's stark separation from local material and energy flows look downright primitive.

Most Western buildings, like high-rises of glass and steel, are designed without a thought for locale. There is, however, a vernacular tradition that can still be drawn on to begin to reconnect the human habitat with the natural world. Vernacular architecture is often thought to be the poor country cousin of "real" architecture—the happenstance outcome of local tinkering right-fully overshadowed by the world's great buildings. As Nicholas Pevsner famously said, "A bicycle shed is a building; a cathedral is architecture." But while we venerate the beauty of our soaring cathedrals and museums, we might also begin to think of vernacular architecture as a rich and evolving aesthetic tradition in its own right, an art that elegantly expresses "the native language of the region."

In the vernacular tradition, good design springs from what fits. In New England, for example, the traditional saltbox house provided shelter from the extremities of the northern winter by responding to what nature allowed and offered. The house was built with a high south wall with many windows to take full advantage of the light of the sun. A steep roof shed driving rain. The hearth was placed in the center of the house so that the warmth radiating from the heated mass of the chimney would not be stolen by bitter winds buffeting the outer walls. On the north side of the house evergreens were planted to further protect it from harsh winter weather. And on the southwest, a maple tree provided shade in the summer and sugar in the spring. The trees became an essential part of the house and the house a part of the landscape. If human artifice is seen as an artifact of nature, they are one.

Working with educator David Orr at Oberlin College, we designed a new environmental studies center that is not only sensitive to locale, but is itself like a tree: a building enmeshed in local energy flows that accrues solar energy, purifies water, and provides habitat for native species. The energy of the sun is collected with rooftop solar cells and pours through southwest-facing windows into a two-story atrium, lighting the public gathering areas. Wastewater is purified by a constructed marshlike ecosystem that breaks down and digests organic material and releases clean, safe water. An earthen berm protects the north side of the center from harsh weather, as do the young trees in the newly planted forest grove, which has begun the long process of reestablishing the habitat of the building's northern Ohio location. And even though the interior feels much like an outdoor classroom—it's lit by the sun and refreshed with fragrant breezes—the students spend much of their time outside tending the garden and orchard. The building offers students and teachers ongoing participation in natural processes.

Perhaps the most moving lesson imparted by the building is that the human presence in the landscape can be regenerative. Not simply benign or less bad, but positive, vital, and good. This is not a rhetorical lesson. At Oberlin, habits of mind grow out of daily interactions with wind, water, soil, and trees; they become the skills and knowledge that inform intelligent design. Those skills can be carried many places, allowing an engagement with the living presence not just of the picturesque or the pastoral but also of a mosaic of extreme landscapes in need of restoration: landfills, crumbling neighborhoods, industrial sites, old cities rent by superhighways. This is the new geography of hope.

On Fifth Avenue in Manhattan, if you look north or south from around 74th Street, you may see sailing over the uptown traffic an enormous red-tailed hawk. Red-tails have been living on the 12th-story ledge of a building on the east side of Fifth Avenue for nearly a decade now, and their nest, a big, shapely tangle of sticks, is visible from the street. If you're lucky, or just patient, you may see the hawks perched on a balcony railing or gliding from the nest on airborne hunts for pigeons and songbirds in nearby Central Park.

It's not what most people expect to find in New York—in fact, it's miraculous to behold—but the hawks are hardly alone in reclaiming a perch in the city. Peregrine falcons, once nearly extinct, nest on skyscrapers and bridges. Egrets, herons, and bitterns have returned to the islands of the East River and New York Harbor. Snowy owls, notes Anne Matthews, a chronicler of wild New York, hunt rabbits along the runways of JFK International Airport. And along with the locals, "migrating birds fly over Manhattan nearly every night of the year."

The presence of wild birds in New York is just the most visible evidence that the city is a complex, evolving ecosystem. A 40-island archipelago where the surge of tidal currents has never ceased, where sea air drifts down Brooklyn subway steps, New York is an organism embedded in nature. Still, the return of wild creatures is a striking reminder. North American cities have always been most strongly connected to the wild and the rural by the flow of raw materials, goods, and waste. As the historian William Cronon tells it, the story of cities is the story of the economic and ecological relationships between a metropolis and its rural hinterland. Typically, a city's economic life transforms the landscape in ways that are not terribly friendly to wild animals, whether they live within urban borders or in the far-off landscapes that are the source of metropolitan wealth. In most cases, the animals aren't moving in, they're moving out.

Consider 19th-century Chicago. In *Nature's Metropolis*, Cronon traces how Chicago's grain, meat, and timber markets transformed the landscape of the West. Railroads, grain elevators, cow pastures, stockyards, feedlots, and wheat farms stretching from Illinois to the Rocky Mountains all emerged in relation to Chicago's markets. All of these landscapes of production created a "gritty web of material connections" that fed, clothed, and sheltered the people of Chicago and its hinterland, many of whom enjoyed the benefits of a thriving culture. But not without cost. The harvest of commodities also created a bevy of "ghost landscapes" on both ends of the rails that carried nature to market. On one end, the overcut white pine forests of Wisconsin, the plowed-under tallgrass prairie, and the slaughter of the bison. On the other, the hovering dark cloud of coal smoke, the stench of meatpacking, the sorrow of tenement dwellings in the Great Gray City. All of which is to say that landscapes rural, urban, wild, and industrial share a common fate: To do well by one, we must do well by all.

We'd like to suggest that each of these landscapes can be a healthy, generative place, a place that allows people and nature to fruitfully co-exist. The industrial revolution is not the model by which we gauge our hopes. The conflicts between nature and industry evident in Chicago's story—the same conflicts that have yielded ghost landscapes all over the world—were not the result of a grand, carefully conceived plan. Instead, they took place gradually as industrialists, engineers, and designers tried to solve problems and take immediate advantage of what they considered to be opportunities in a period of massive and rapid change. Few foresaw the exhaustion of the Earth's resources or appreciated the true beneficence of its natural systems. The ways in which natural resources were used to produce goods reflected the spirit of the day—and yielded a host of unintended, yet tragic consequences. Today, design can reflect our growing knowledge of the living Earth, allowing participation in landscape that not only renews our engagement with the natural world, but restores the land itself.

Conception of place is the foundation of ecological intelligence. With Earth in mind, our relation to the landscapes we use changes dramatically. Consider, for example, the Menomonee of Wisconsin, a tribe that has been harvesting wood for generations using a method of logging that allows forests to thrive. Conventional logging operations, like those that cut timber during Chicago's boom years, are focused on the single-purpose, utilitarian goal of producing a certain amount of wood pulp. Little attention is given to nesting birds, the diversity of microorganisms in the soil, or the headwater streams that emerge in the shadows of the forest canopy. The result is a clear-cut landscape devoid of the rich diversity of life. The Menomonee, on the other hand, principally cut only the weaker trees, leaving the strong mother trees and preserving connectivity in the upper canopy for birds and arboreal animals. On the ground, the living system of the forest also remains intact. There is sunlight and shade, the nutrient cycles are uninterrupted, and water flows from the land as it has for generations. The forest remains a forest, a celebration of abundance and biota, shadow and life.

This strategy has been enormously productive. In the 1870s, the Menomonee identified 1.3 billion standing board feet of timber—what, in the timber industry, is tellingly known as stumpage—on a 235,000-acre reservation. Over the years they have harvested 2.25 billion board feet and there are 1.7 billion standing. One might say they have figured out what the forest can productively offer them.

Industry, too, can be a regenerative force. When designers employ the intelligence of natural systems—the abundance of the sun's energy, the effectiveness of nutrient cycling—both factories and manufactured products can nourish rather than deplete the world. We are currently leading a team restoring an industrial site, for example, that at one time would have been abandoned. Built more than 75 years ago, the site was one of the most productive in the world. By the end of the 20th century, however, it had become a brownfield, a sprawling wasteland of dilapidated buildings, leaky pipes, and old equipment. The land was contaminated, bare of all but the most persistent vegetation, and a nearby river was badly polluted. The company could have fenced off the site and built a new factory where land and labor are cheap. Instead, it decided to transform it into a healthy, productive, life-supporting place.

The new plant we're designing will feature skylights for daylighting the factory floor and a roof covered with growing plants. The "living roof" will provide habitat for birds, insects, and microorganisms and, in concert with porous paving and a series of constructed wetlands and swales, will control and filter storm water runoff. Native grasses and other plants will be used to rid the soil of contaminants, and thousands of trees will be planted to create habitat for songbirds and aid in the bio-remediation. It is a landscape of renewal.

No gesture of restoration is trivial. Yet renewing the industrial landscape is certainly deepened when all the ways in which we use energy and materials are in harmony with the larger patterns of life. That's why we've begun to create products designed with the same care as the ecologically intelligent factories that manufacture them, products made with materials that, like the blossoms of a fruit tree, provide nourishment for something new after each useful life. The carpeting used in the Oberlin College building, for example, is leased from a manufacturer that will retrieve and reuse the materials for new, high-quality carpets.

The upholstery fabric used for the auditorium chairs is biodegradable; when the fabric needs to be replaced it is removed from the frame of the chair and becomes food for the garden. We call these discrete material loops the "technical metabolism" and the "biological metabolism," and their elements, biological and technical "nutrients." When all manufactured products and materials are designed as nutrients that flow in these closed-loop cycles, we will be able to celebrate, rather than lament, the human ecological footprint.

Imagine the fruits of such a shift on a large scale. Imagine a garden metropolis, a city of buildings like trees. To begin, even a single building like a tree in an urban neighborhood could spark a meaningful transformation. In communities with an industrial past, such as Brooklyn's Red Hook and Gowanus neighborhoods, a building designed to be part of nature provides a place for residents to experience firsthand the natural processes that sustain life.

In the 19th century Red Hook and Gowanus, like old Chicago, nature came to market. In the 1850s, in fact, the warehouses on the Brooklyn waterfront stored for shipment to foreign markets the grain grown in Chicago's hinterland and shipped east via the Erie Canal. In Brooklyn, the grain barges traveled the Gowanus Canal, formerly a creek that meandered through the wetlands of the Red Hook peninsula. Markets and fortunes changed, but the neighborhoods have nearly always been both a hardscrabble town and an industrial vortex, drawing refineries, factories, shipyards, and Robert Moses' elevated freeways. It's not an easy place to garden.

Yet, as in Manhattan, there is an emerging sense that nature has a place here. The sprawling rooftops of the old warehouses are wonderful places to invite her return. Blue crabs and pink jellyfish have already returned to the beleaguered canal, the first living creatures seen in the Gowanus in decades. People are returning to the docks, not only to work in new commercial ventures, but to fish, stroll, and watch the waters of Upper New York Bay. A conventional developer might see this landscape as empty, ripe for taking and making; an ecologist might see that it is full of life and possibility. Why not enhance the local web of life? Why not cultivate an urban agricultural district on the rooftops of Red Hook and Gowanus, a network of public gardens that makes visible the vital connections between water, soil, food, and human culture?

The residents of Gowanus have already begun to do so. An old soap factory a couple of blocks from the canal has been converted into a thriving arts center, and plans call for ongoing renovations to the building that will make it even more of a community hub. A rooftop garden will be planted with wildflowers, herbs, and vegetables. Neighbors will tend the garden, producing food for their families and for the children who attend after-school dance classes in the studio housed below, where the windows open wide and the air is sometimes touched with the scent of the sea. While solar panels harvest the power of the sun, cisterns will collect rainwater. Even the building's wastewater will flow in cycles; it will be purified by an indoor botanical garden on the ground floor and reused to water the garden, a profoundly meaningful process in a neighborhood that once flushed its sewage into the canal. Over a day, over a year, over a lifetime, sense and gesture in this small garden world will reveal the living layers of landscape.

It may be years before buildings like trees, rooftop gardens, and the return of birds and wildflowers, block by block, reshape the urban landscape. Years, too, before intelligence and attention and the work of our hands heal our rivers, forests, farmlands, and small towns. But the renewal of an old conversation with the natural world has begun. By our own intentions and by grace we will grow more fluent. This is the work and the pleasure of generations to come. Through it we will find our way home and realize, as we grow ever more aware of our place in the landscape, that we have been home all along.

Valley and snowy peaks, Himalaya MARIA STENZEL

reflections in a hidden land ✳ GEORGE B. SCHALLER

THE WATERS OF THE YARLUNG TSANGPO in southeastern Tibet rush into the deepest gorge in the world. On one side of the river is 25,446-foot Namcha Barwa and on the other, a mere 15 miles away, is 23,461-foot Gyala Pelri. As it thunders northward through that gorge, the river then makes a large bend and heads southward into India. We turn east away from the river and climb a spur of Namche Barwa toward a pass, the Doxiong La.

My three Chinese co-workers—Zhang Hong, Endi Zhang, and Lu Zhi—and I are here under the auspices of the Tibet Forestry Department to make an ecological survey. With terrain that includes habitats from rain forests at 3,000 feet upward to glaciers within a few miles, the flora and fauna are extraordinarily rich. Isolated behind snow ranges without road access and virtually closed to outsiders because of its proximity to the disputed border with India, this region, generally known as Medog or Motuo, has been little visited. Recently it was given protection as the 3,600-square-mile Yarlung Tsangpo Great Canyon National Reserve. With 15,000 people, mostly Monpa, Lopa, and Tibetan, living in 114 villages, the reserve is under considerable human pressure, and it is our task to evaluate this impact on the wildlife and forests.

We toil upward, with 18 porters trailing behind, as we leave the stands of fir and birch and then rhododendron thickets until only snow slopes and ice faces are ahead. It is mid-May 2000, and the passes into Medog are open only from now until October. We reach the Doxiong La, a mere 14,000 feet high; there is grandeur in its desolation. An avalanche rumbles in the distance. Standing at this convergence of snow and sky, I lift my face and feel like a passing cloud. Spirits soar in such infinite space and the silence speaks to the soul. The mind has a heightened sense of awareness and clarity. Mountains are said to be the abodes of distant gods. But at moments such as this they become intimate, offering communion and unity with the natural world. I have since read that during transcendent experiences, such as during meditation, brain activity is affected in that some neural traffic to the cortex is shut down. As a result the brain ceases to make a distinction between self and the environment.

We cannot tarry and so descend, filled with expectation, toward a basin and a shadowy canyon beyond. Snow soon gives way to a sodden slope with purple primulas in bloom. Two monal pheasants glide singing downslope. That evening I stand by my tent beyond the circle of light from the two campfires and look at the luminous peaks beneath a sliver of moon. I am restless, a wanderer at the edge of the known. We have come to make a record of the area, but our visit is fleeting, only a month. We will visit these mountains but not inhabit them.

The mind shapes a landscape, giving it meaning beyond its reality. Herman Melville expressed this feeling of place: "It is not down on any map; true places never are." I can describe the visible portions of a landscape, its mountains and forests; I can even embrace its mythic concepts, finding glory in peaks and value in wilderness. However, I am also aware of a cultural void in my perceptions: I lack an awareness of the hidden and intangible forces, the spiritual geography of this and other regions. I would have to see with different eyes and hear with different ears to define the landscape, as local people do.

Many cultures are dependent on a sacred landscape as part of their value system. Australian Aborigines have their song lines, a labyrinth of invisible paths, the tracks of ancestors. India and Japan have sacred groves of native vegetation. Amerindians have a strong spiritual tradition of nature mysticism. And the Buddhist Himalaya has its hidden lands, a visionary landscape of remote sanctuaries, or *beyul*. Two American scholars of Tibetan culture, Ian Baker and Hamid Sardar, first made me aware of these hidden lands. Now, in Medog, I know that we have just entered one, Dechen Pemako, the Lotus of Great Bliss.

In the eighth century the Indian sage Padmasambhava, the Lotus-Born, visited Tibet and established Buddhism by converting powerful and belligerent deities and demons into protectors of the new faith. During his wanderings in the Himalaya he created beyul hidden among the towering peaks. These sanctuaries were places of inner peace and outer tranquillity, earthly paradises so lovely and filled with mysterious power that no one would ever want to leave. They were also refuges in time of calamity. Padmasambhara wrote guidebooks to the beyul and secreted them, knowing that those of faith would find them at critical times and decipher them. Legends of these fabled hidden lands sent Tibetan lamas into the wilderness in search of them. Pemako was identified in the 17th century. As predicted over a millennium earlier, Pemako became a refuge for people in times of strife, most recently during the turbulent 1950s, when China took control of Tibet.

Tropical warmth wraps around us as we descend. Austere hemlock and fir give way to lush broad-leaved forests with orchid-laden branches, tree ferns, and wild bananas. Land leeches hump over moldering leaves in marvelous abundance. They help me to redefine paradise. Ian Baker quotes a lama as saying, "When leeches infest your legs, think of them as drawing out all Karmic impurities." Still, leeches, malarial mosquitoes, gnats, fleas, landslides, incessant downpours, and unstable trails along cliffs make the spiritual context of this hidden land elusive to an outsider. Each beyul consists of three parts. The first is the outer, visible portion of which I am all too aware. The second is the inner symbolic region with all the memories and myths of deities, demons, and spirits, which is beyond my power to see. Finally there is the heart—a secret dimension, the door to paradise—which must be discovered through merit.

To travel through Pemako is to move through the body of the female deity Vajrayogini. The mystery of her form and her wisdom will be revealed to a pilgrim. Gyala Pelri symbolizes her head, Namcha Barwa and Kangla Karpo her breasts, the Doxiong La her hips, and the Rinchenpung temple her navel, the center of bliss. Coursing through her body is a central energy channel, the Yarlung Tsangpo.

We reach the Yarlung Tsangpo again after a four-day hike and cross the river on a hanging bridge to the village of Beibeng. Here in the main valley and various tributary valleys the ancient forests are mostly gone. Flat areas have been converted to paddies. The Monpa and Lopa practice slash-and-burn cultivation. The forest is cut down, burned, and a crop, usually maize, planted for a year or two. Then the field is abandoned and soon grows into a thicket and scrubby forest. Meanwhile more pristine forest is cleared, often on very steep slopes causing erosion and landslides. Wildlife, we learn, is much hunted in Pemako, and some species have become rare. Musk deer is prized for its musk, which is used in traditional medicines, and barking deer, takin, red goral, Assamese macaque, and black bears are killed for meat and hides. The last tigers in Tibet, no more than perhaps 20, live in Pemako, but with wild prey decimated, they kill livestock and are in turn reviled by the local people. Although the difference between Buddhist precepts and practice about the sanctity of and compassion for life is considerable in Pemako, the human population is still low and wildlife does survive in remote forest tracts. The door to paradise remains open.

We travel north along the Yarlung Tsangpo to the town of Medog. Above, hidden in the hills, is Rinchenpung, Vajrayogini's navel. After a climb of 3,500 feet, we reach a bowl in the hills. At its bottom is a marsh surrounded by bamboo, and on a rise is a squat, three-tiered temple, ocher and white, surrounded by poles on which prayer flags snap in the wind. Seven Tibetan families live here, growing barley and millet as they meditate in this place of exceptional spiritual power.

The temple is closed; no monks or nuns are in residence. But a one-handed, elderly caretaker opens the massive door for us. Inside the main room is an angry figure of Padmasambhara subduing evil spirits, several demonic masks, a few small bronze statues of deities, a shelf of books. The temple has been destroyed twice in recent years—by an earthquake in 1950 and during the Cultural Revolution in the late 1960s—and then rebuilt, yet it has an aura of old age and neglect rather than a place where sky spirits dance and sing. Passionate pilgrims, young and old, still travel here from afar to purify their perceptions, braving all adversity put in their paths by demons. It reminded me that the spiritual significance of a site does not depend on an imposing structure created by humans.

It also reminded me that mountaineers sometimes profane the gods and anger local people out of ignorance or indifference by trampling on sacred summits. Climbers in the U.S. persist in ascending Ship Rock, a site holy to the Navajo. A Japanese team tried to climb sacred Kawa Karpo in eastern Tibet. Thousands of Tibetans are said to have prayed that the team would not succeed. All 17 climbers died in an avalanche. Bhutan closed its high summits because of one team's surreptitious attempt at holy Gangkar Punsum. And in a recent example of gross insensitivity, a Spanish team planned to climb Mount Kailash, sacred to Tibetan Buddhists, Hindus, and Bon.

All 8,000-meter peaks have been climbed, as have most 7,000-meter ones, and now the scramble for those of 6,000 meters has begun. Surely a few sacred summits can be spared an assault with cramponed boots and instead be shown reverence—not only by local people but also by tourists, trekkers, and trophy climbers—as sublime symbols of beauty, compassion, and human restraint. After all, many mountaineers are on quests similar to those of pilgrims, in search of liberation and deeper perceptions. To ignore the sacred, to violate the dignity of local people, is to degrade the ethical values of a culture and diminish it.

Pemako shows a discordance between ecological and Buddhist principles. This is even more apparent in another hidden land, Kyimolung, the Valley of Bliss, secluded in the fastness of the Himalaya. On a trip in 1999, Hamid Sardar and I traveled together. It was March and the sky was hazy from fires sweeping through conifer forests. With casual vandalism, villagers were destroying the last forests upon which they depend for fuel and timber. When asked why they destroyed, they replied with the desolate words, "We have always burned." These Tibetans live in smoke-blackened huts, respiratory and other diseases are common, children are often malnourished, and family planning does not exist. Land is already too scarce to support the population. Spiritual salvation is ultimately linked to a healthy environment. So far we have seen no sign of an earthly paradise in Kyimolung.

Surely the inner secret sanctum of Kyimolung will have retained its tranquillity, hidden as it is in a small valley accessible only by a perilous route through a canyon. Days of trekking bring us to a temple, which I shall call Sertang, the Gold Mandala, because the lama wants to keep its location secret. The temple is flanked by torrents, is tucked against a forest, and has a backdrop of sheer cliffs streaked with snow. Here, it seems, the human and divine can merge. But we are distraught to find not a quiet retreat for contemplation, as in generations past, but a major construction project to create a monastery for monks and nuns. Huge hemlocks, more than 200 years old, are being felled for a few roof shingles and the rest left to rot. Sertang is too small and fragile to support such a scale of development, both ecologically and spiritually; its harmony is being destroyed.

The lama meets with us. His mouth is taut when we ask him why he protects the Himalayan tahr in the area so well that these wild goats feed around his temple as tame as domestic ones, yet destroys the forests carelessly. He replies, "Trees don't meditate." Plants are not considered sentient by most Buddhist sects, although such trees as the banyan and flowers as the lotus have symbolic significance. The lama may view this hidden land in a certain divine way, but he lacks ecological understanding of the landscape. Indeed, this was also true of all others, lama and layman alike, we met on our travels. Religious conviction about the sanctity of life does not include ecological awareness, as I had naively assumed.

Other religions also glorify the scriptures and neglect reality. As stated in the Holy Koran, "Allah loveth not wasters." In Christianity and Judaism, humans are viewed as stewards of all life as divinely willed by the Creator. Indeed, God delegated Noah to implement the first endangered species act by taking every kind of animal, two by two, onto his ark. Hinduism proclaims a bond with the rhythms of nature; "conserve or perish" is the message of the *Bhagavad Gita.* Other religions also incorporate respect for life into their teachings. China's Confucian philosophy stresses harmony with nature as well, using the phrase *tian ren he yi,* "nature and humankind into one whole." In recent years an effort has been made to forge an alliance between religion and conservation. The Assisi Declaration in 1986 affirmed the unity of humankind with nature. The National Religious Partnership for the Environment in North America urged its congregations in 1994 to integrate environmental concerns into worship. Small but important steps. However, the major task ahead is to raise the ecological awareness of all monks and mullahs, of shamans and priests, so that they can educate those of their faiths.

A new spiritual awakening eluded me in the hidden lands of the Himalaya, but the travels did offer greater understanding as well as useful reflections. Paradise must be regained, though not just through visions and merit, as the ancient guidebooks instruct. There must also be a commitment to protect the landscape and a recognition that all animals and plants have intrinsic worth. In this way the hidden lands could provide guidance to all humankind: They could show the way to spiritual and ecological enlightenment. Hidden lands no doubt persist in all faiths. But no visionaries in the future will be able to find their treasures if the land is destroyed now.

I still find hope in these mountains. I remember the morning when Hamid and I leave Sertang. The tracks of a leopard head toward the inner sanctum. There, near the temple, it will hunt Himalayan tahr as ordained by the sacred ordering of nature. Its continued presence is a vivid reminder that Kyimolung remains basically intact. With renewed awareness and compassion it can endure. It remains, like many others, a valley of hope.

Ordessa National Park, Spain JIM THORSELL

peaks, parks, and peace ✳ JIM THORSELL

Where Nature's Geography Collides

There is much comfort in high hills
And a great easing of the heart.
We look upon them, and our nature fills
With loftier images from their life apart.
They set our feet on curves of freedom bent
To snap the circles of our discontent.

GEOFFREY WINTHROP YOUNG

MANY FARSIGHTED AUTHORS have portrayed a transcendence, a spiritual solace that gives deeper meaning to their experiences in the high hills. Legions of orophiles speak of mountains as places of refuge, renewal, and recreation. And for indigenous groups living in mountain regions, nearby peaks often take on sacred status.

That mountains evoke such a cross-cultural aesthetic response partially explains why such a high proportion of the world's terrestrial parks have been established in alpine regions. Indeed, some 40 percent of the area of the planet's protected regions are found in mountain biomes. This nearly 750 million acres of the world's prime real estate is equivalent in size to Alaska and British Columbia combined.

Analyzing more closely where mountain parks are located, it becomes evident that many of them are in remote locations, often at the frontiers of nations. In turn, many of these parks straddle two or more international frontiers and become what IUCN, the World Conservation Union, classifies as trans-boundary protected areas. The most recent tally of these amounts to 33 pairs of mountain parks involving 44 countries. There are biological, economic, and political advantages when designating contiguous protected areas as trans-boundary parks. Emerging as a strategic force for global security are "parks for peace." Indeed, a number of peace parks have been established, at least in part, to help resolve conflicts between countries, as well as to create economic opportunities and support biodiversity conservation.

The belief behind peace parks is that good borders can make good neighbors. Instead of collision at disputed frontiers, it is possible to have collusion. But can mountain parks, which provide peace to the human soul, also foster peace and cooperation between countries? Real-life examples from six disparate trans-boundary mountain parks demonstrate where and how they are contributing, not only to peace and stability, but also to more effective conservation management.

※

WATERTON/GLACIER INTERNATIONAL PEACE PARK (CANADA/U.S.A.): Almost 200 years have passed since Canada and the United States have had a military confrontation, so, at first blush, a peace park along their borders appears to be only a symbolic gesture. In fact, the designation as the world's first officially declared international peace park has come to mean a great deal more. The original declaration in 1932 by the Canadian Parliament and the U.S. Congress dedicated the two parks for the purpose of commemorating the long-existing close relationship between the two countries. Since then, cooperation in jointly managing the area has grown and led to a broader understanding for all protected areas on their mutual borders. By being the first of a kind, Waterton/Glacier also has served as a model for the creation of others.

✳

LA AMISTAD INTERNATIONAL PARK (COSTA RICA/PANAMA): The rugged Talamanca Mountains, which form the border between these two countries, were the subject of a joint presidential declaration in 1979 made expressly to foster protection of the highly diverse natural and cultural heritage of the region and to serve as a model for peace and friendship between neighboring countries (*amistad* means "friendship"). In addition to neutralizing a potential border conflict between the two countries, the creation of an international park has stimulated a number of related peace initiatives in Central America. Notable among these was in the San Juan River Basin shared by Nicaragua and Costa Rica, once an area caught up in the Sandinista contra war. A cooperation agreement entitled *"Si-A-Paz"* (translated meaning Yes to Peace) has led to the establishment of the Mesoamerican biological corridor project to link a network of parks through the region.

LOS KATÍOS/DARIEN NATIONAL PARKS (COLOMBIA/PANAMA): The Darien region at the isthmus of Panama is the meeting point of North and South America and a hot spot of biodiversity. The original impetus for establishing the two parks, however, was to create an "inspection zone" to control the spread of foot-and-mouth disease into Central America. This buffer function has also proved useful in addressing the problems of illegal drug trafficking and the guerrilla war in Colombia. Park agencies from the two countries work together to coordinate their management and to maintain an uneasy stability in the region.

✳

CORDILLERA DEL CONDOR (ECUADOR/PERU): In 1998, international mediation of this long-running border dispute resulted in a treaty to reduce tensions on the area. Included in the treaty is the provision for a peace park in part of the area inhabited by over 100,000 indigenous residents. It is perhaps premature to forecast the effectiveness of this action, but it illustrates the use of the peace park concept to address a geopolitical conflict.

✳

MALOTI/DRAKENSBERG TRANSFRONTIER CONSERVATION AREA (LESOTHO/SOUTH AFRICA): After 20 years of study and negotiation, a Memorandum of Understanding was signed by the respective ministers of environments early in 2001 to formalize an integrated approach to this area. The MoU makes a specific reference to the linkage between peace and economic development and environmental protection. Under this general framework, several peace parks will be established in one of southern Africa's most dramatic landscapes. In addition to fostering closer collaboration in water management, degraded-land restoration, and control of cattle rustling, the project has leveraged significant funding support from the World Bank and the Peace Parks Foundation.

✳

Mont Perdu World Heritage Site (France/Spain): Mont Perdu, Monte Perdido in Spanish, is generally regarded as the culmination of the Pyrenees Mountains, which form the border between France and Spain. It is protected on the French side by the Pyrenee National Park and in Spain by Ordessa National Park. In order to satisfy the stringent requirements for its joint inscription on the World Heritage List, the two countries set up special management arrangements to ensure closer collaboration. These included a special charter and a joint management committee. Cross-border ties between staff and a concerted effort to harmonize tourism policies have markedly improved since its successful designation in 1997. Mont Perdu is just one of a dozen trans-frontier mountain parks in Europe, but it is the only one that has achieved World Heritage status.

So far, so good. These six examples from four continents demonstrate how trans-border mountain parks help resolve border conflicts, assist in rural development, and strengthen site management efforts. Cooperation in nature conservation also helps open the doors between nations to address issues other than the environment. Not by chance, all of the sites discussed are on the World Heritage List, and all are distinguished by having formal cooperation agreements in place. It is hard to argue against using parks to foster and reinforce conservation, peace, and humanitarian agendas.

✳

NOW THE CHALLENGE. Pick up any newspaper these days, and the prospects for extending the concept of peace parks to other areas will quickly become apparent. Certainly the world could use all the initiatives it can muster to promote peace, sustainable development, and environmental protection. Although peace parks are only one tool, they may well prove worth pursuing in several other selected mountain sites.

✳

THE KARAKORAM MOUNTAINS (ON THE BORDER OF PAKISTAN AND INDIA): It is hard to imagine a more inhospitable and unlikely theater for a war than the Siachen Glacier area in the eastern Karakoram. But since 1984, when hostilities broke out between Pakistan and India over boundary demarcation in the far north corner of Kashmir, a military campaign has raged intermittently. By 2001, 3,500 soldiers had died—most due to high-altitude-related problems, not gunfire. The area has become littered with abandoned military hardware; wildlife has been extirpated, forests cut for firewood, and streams contaminated.

All this in one of the most spectacular natural areas on the planet—7,000-meter-high peaks and one of the longest valley glaciers (45 miles) outside the polar regions. The political situation remains at an impasse, but both governments are reportedly seeking some form of resolution. Within India numerous but ineffective letters in national media from conservationists and the mountaineering community have called for the peace park concept to be considered.

As a contribution to the International Year of the Mountain in 2002, IUCN is also attempting to bring the two sides together to at least call an armistice and begin work to connect Pakistan's Central Karakoram National Park with a matching area in the Saltoro Valley. This is an issue for the two individual countries to solve, but prospects for this happening are not good. Still, as the Pakistani scholar Mahbub ul Haq once said: "We may fail. But we can never forgive ourselves for not trying."

＊

THE ALTAI MOUNTAINS (RUSSIA, CHINA, MONGOLIA, AND KAZAKHSTAN): The Altai mountain range is a biologically and ethnically diverse area of over 37 million acres that straddles the border of these 4 countries. A dozen border parks exist in the region, including two that are on the World Heritage List. With assistance from the German Federal Agency for Nature Protection, the Russian government has set up the Altai Convention for Sustainable Development, which aims to establish an international biosphere reserve over the region.

Local people have indicated they are interested in peace parks only if they can contribute to promoting tourism to assist a struggling local economy. With proposals for oil pipelines and new roads through the region, nature conservation is going to need all the help it can get as it confronts a push for major industrial developments.

❊

The Northern Annamite Range (Laos and Vietnam): 2.5 million acres of forest is included in a series of protected areas that run along the international boundary of these two countries. Management of them is rudimentary and is complicated by the legacy of previous wars—unexploded bombs and land mines. The existence of minority cultures that migrate across boundaries, as well as proposals for large hydroelectric dams, further complicate regional planning in the area. To catalyze closer relations and to work toward a system of border parks, an Indochina Biodiversity Forum coordinated by the World Wildlife Federation (WWF) was set up in 1993. By bringing together wildlife and parks officials from both countries, substantial progress has been achieved in reducing the level of suspicions between the two countries. The end product of a peace park along the Ho Chi Minh Trail, however, is still some years away.

❊

The Qoomolangma/Sagarmatha region (China/Nepal): The ecosystem around Mount Everest is an extraordinary depository of biological and cultural diversity. Much of the area is protected in the contiguous Nepalese national parks of Sagarmatha, Langtang, and Makalu-Barun, and the Qoomolangma Reserve in China. Opportunities for cooperation in conservation and sustainable development have been supported by various donors over the past decade with the objective of harmonizing the various approaches between the two countries. A formal peace park declaration around the highest point on Earth would facilitate this cooperation and send an important signal to the world that Everest is not just about climbing.

✳

THE RWENZORI/VIRUNGA (CONGO/UGANDA/RWANDA): Another area that has presented seemingly intractable conservation, security, and humanitarian problems is the Great Lakes/Virunga Volcano region of central Africa. The heavy pressure on natural habitats from an especially dense human population combined with poverty, civil war, and refugee flows has taken a heavy toll on the three countries that share an outstanding, but degraded, network of parks.

Faced with such a multitude of problems, in 1991 a consortium of conservation groups formed the International Gorilla Conservation Programme (IGCP), which has maintained a field presence in the area through these troubled times. Part of their approach has been to propose a peace park in the region based both on conservation and political and diplomatic rationales. Using the peace park as a "prestigious pole of attraction," the IGCP hopes to attract donor funds, coordinate management efforts of the three countries, and use the concept as a tool for political stabilization of the region. A feasibility study has been conducted, and a draft of a formal agreement between the three governments has been prepared. The IGCP, however, admits that mutual confidence of the partners is still lacking, and continuing security problems preclude further progress.

✳

KANCHENJUNGA CONSERVATION AREA (NEPAL/INDIA/CHINA): Kanchen-junga 28,210 feet (8,598 meters), in the eastern Himalaya, is the world's third highest peak. The slopes of the mountain have been severely degraded over the past half century by overharvesting of medicinal plants as well as slash-and-burn agriculture. To address the problem, senior representatives from the three affected countries formulated a plan that would establish a tri-national peace park around the mountain. Contiguous multiple-use protected areas have been established in Nepal and in Sikkim, and another is being considered for the Tibet Autonomous Region. Collaboration has begun toward controlling illegal trade and poaching across the international boundaries, and an integrated approach to managing growing tourism is being formulated. If China becomes a fully committed partner, Kanchenjunga could become the model peace park in the region.

✳

THE SOUTH-CENTRAL ANDES (CHILE/ARGENTINA): The frontier between these two countries has long been the scene of sovereignty struggles and border skirmishes. Now that an international boundary commission has ruled on the dispute, tensions have eased, and a peace park to commemorate the settlement has been suggested. Several prospective sites are feasible. One is the Los Glaciares/Torres del Paine/Bernando O'Higgins parks complex in southern Patagonia. A second is the contiguous border parks of Lanín/Nahuel Huapi (Argentina) and Puye-hue/Vicente Perez Rosales (Chile). A third prospect is a 600,000 hectare area including Lake Jeinimeni National Park in Chile with the Sol de Mayo area in Argentina, recently purchased privately by the Conservation Land Trust. Designation of any one, or even all three, of these areas as a peace park would underline the growing cooperation between two countries sharing a spectacular alpine region.

Making any of these seven potential trans-frontier mountain parks bring about peace is not going to be easy, and these efforts are going to come at a price. Governments in most of the above countries lack the financial resources to invest in remote, sparsely inhabited mountain regions. Some countries will see implied threats to national sovereignty and balk at solutions imposed from outside. But better today to invest modest sums on pursuing the stabilizing benefits that trans-border cooperation can bring than face significantly higher social costs of alternative scenarios. Perhaps this is what Thoreau meant when he claimed that "in wildness is the preservation of the world."

※

WITH THE ABOVE EXAMPLES, as well as with other remnant transborder parks around the planet in need of attention, what is being done to protect the wildness that remains? Fortunately, lots. Some initiatives are seeking strategic benefits through peace negotiations while others are focusing on achieving regional integration and securing landscape-scale conservation.

The peace park movement is thus spreading. The rationale for it has been vividly summed up by South Africa's former minister of environment at a recent IUCN conference on the topic:

> *The rivers of Southern Africa are shared by more*
> *than one country. Our mountain ranges do not end*

abruptly because some 19th century politician drew a line on a map. The winds, the oceans, the rain and atmospheric currents do not recognize political frontiers. The earth's environment is the common property of all humanity and creation, and what takes place in one country affects not only its neighbours, but many others well beyond its borders.

As was the case with the world's first international peace park at Waterton/Glacier, where Rotary Clubs led the way, many of the initiatives are being spearheaded by nongovernmental organizations. Impressive progress has been made in the southern Africa region by the Peace Parks Foundation, which has raised millions of dollars to help create peace parks between Mozambique, Botswana, Lesotho, and South Africa. The International Mountaineering and Climbing Federation, with backing from its 10 million members, is actively lobbying governments to proceed with trans-border parks in the Karakoram mountains and around Mont Blanc.

IUCN has sponsored expert workshops and published a number of technical publications on the topic, providing examples of bilateral cooperative agreements, best-practice guidelines, and codes of conduct. IUCN is also working with the United Nations University for Peace and other partners to establish a Global Partnership for Peace Parks to catalyze the growing interest and pursue donor support. UNESCO's (The United Nations Educational, Scientific and Cultural Organization's) Man and the Biosphere Programme is pursuing "trans-border biosphere reserves" that will reinforce its goals of preserving biocultural diversity while providing models of land management and strengthening research and training activities. And various governments have signed bilateral agreements that ensure their shared "wildness" is effectively protected.

Zermatt, Switzerland JAMES P. BLAIR

european mountain decalogue   ✳ REINHOLD MESSNER

EUROPEAN MOUNTAINS, as well as sharing the same climatic and geographic variety, and being the location of rest and recreation resorts,
more importantly share similar socio-economic structures representing a unifying element within the European Union (EU). By
my definition of European Mountains, I include those more than
500 m above sea level: the Alps, Apennines, Pyrenees, Sierra
Nevada, Carpathians, the mountains of Great Britain, France, Italy,
Belgium, Germany, Switzerland, Austria, the Czech Republic, Slo-
vakia, Spain and Portugal, the Dinaric Alps and the mountains of
Scandinavia, Greece and Bulgaria.

The fundamental importance of mountain areas in today's

EU, as well as in the future enlarged Union, should not be defined merely by problems, but also, and more importantly, for the numerous merits these mountain regions represent. They are a water and water energy resource, a land of peculiar ecosystems and biodiversity, the ideal place for rest, tranquillity and for recovering physical strength. Their open spaces stimulate the imagination, are full of diversified cultural realities and identities, as well as farming resources; traditional breeds of domestic animals, edible, aromatic and medicinal plants etc.

Mountain areas cover one third of the entire EU surface area. Although there are many specific local challenges in mountain communities, their inhabitants also share similar possible solutions to problems that are common to many mountain areas. A global and transboundary perspective is needed, one which respects sustainability and employment needs. Only in this way will it be possible to safeguard each mountain area's peculiar characteristics, as well as assure livelihoods for the local population and places of recreation, regeneration and relaxation used primarily by the inhabitants of urban centres. What is now at stake is the protection of mountain areas as living space.

The "decalogue of values" for mountain areas discussed in 2002—declared International Year of the Mountain—should stimulate the creation of an adequate framework within the EU that reaffirms the vital importance of all mountain areas. The framework could look like this:

European mountain areas are a cluster of small landscape realities with a strong cultural heritage shaped and tended over thousands of years of human effort. They possess a number of extraordinary high mountain landscapes representing a unique and indivisible richness.

The maintenance and care of EU mountain regions benefits all European—and international—populations. In fact, these mountains are a water resource, a place of leisure and relaxation, an area producing highly nutritious and healthy food, as well as a "green" lung—an unpolluted air resource. These benefits are enjoyed by the densely inhabited areas nearby, the entire EU territory, and the world at large and, as such, need to be protected.

The presence of stable, local, mountain communities, who autonomously and adequately structure and organise their own territories, is a fundamental and crucial prerequisite for all of those activities needed to conserve mountain rural landscapes.

The value of high altitude territories above tree level, only recently made accessible to tourists thanks to modern infrastructures, is to be found in their open spaces, in the silence of their magnificent and uncontaminated landscapes as well as in the risks they present.

These values, though apparently unpractical, must be seriously considered, and not merely because they are becoming increasingly rare within the EU. The integrity of high altitude territories must be conserved, as this will be irreparably lost if the building of infrastructures doesn't stop. Thus it is imperative that we stop building additional, high altitude infrastructures. In fact, people should be encouraged to reach these areas under their own steam, autonomously and responsibly, without leaving behind lasting traces of their passing. With full respect for the environment, they would then better understand how to appreciate uncontaminated nature and protect areas that are continuously at risk.

Only a policy of decentralised settlements, orientated towards the sustainable use of mountain areas below tree line, can make mountain regions achievable, accessible and practical, thus creating the basic conditions for tourism, physical rehabilitation and appreciation of Nature. To guarantee a decent quality of life for the local populations, it is also necessary that transit routes are build so as to minimise noise pollution and all other forms of contamination resulting from excessive traffic in narrow constricted valleys and passes.

The key to protecting the mountain areas is a contextual approach. This should take into account the challenges faced by the local communities, landscape conservation problems and respect for their cultural heritage, plus the need to protect the mountains from invasive infrastructures. These are the imperative issues that need to be addressed to ensure that mountains are a viable resource in the long-term. The combination of ecological agriculture and tourism is the key to sustainable local development. Interregional co-operation among mountain regions should be promoted and increased, and considerable self-rule should be created and recognised by the EU institutions.

The only way to guarantee the sustainability of mountain populations and promote the awareness of the values they preserve through personal identification with their areas, is through the conservation of the regional cultural heritage, the landscape and unparalleled beauty of the mountain views.

There is a strong interrelationship between mountain regions and highly inhabited centres. Mountains have the capacity to protect lowlands and towns from natural disasters. In the EU document entitled European Spatial Development Perspective (ESDP), the EU has established that, in order to guarantee sustainable development, Europe needs an economic and housing structure leading to "balanced exploitation of space." An increase in the depopulation of mountain areas and the resulting concentration of population in urban areas can only have negative consequences.

That is why the EU introduces the necessary measures to counter this form of development.

Because of the peculiar socio-economic conditions of the local population, many non-EU mountain regions, which are often situated far from inhabited centres, face other sorts of problems than those we have in Europe. However, the opportunity lies in the limited number of useful applications for the solutions that European models have developed to date, for other international mountain communities situated near large urban communities.

Machu Picchu, Peru WADE DAVIS

culture at the edge · WADE DAVIS

IN NORTHWEST BRITISH COLUMBIA, a year or so after graduating from college, I was hired as one of the first park rangers in the Spatsizi Wilderness, a roadless track of two million acres in the remote reaches of the Cassiar Mountains. The job description was deliciously vague: wilderness assessment and public relations. In two long seasons, our ranger team—myself and one other, Al Poulsen, a six-foot-four vegetarian who grazed through meals and could conjure golden eagles out of the wild—encountered perhaps a dozen visitors. Wilderness assessment was a license to explore the park at will, tracking game and mapping the horse trails of outfitters, describing routes up mountains and down rivers, recording what we could of the movements of large populations of caribou and sheep, mountain goats, grizzly bears, and wolves.

In the course of these wanderings, we came upon an old native gravesite on an open bench overlooking Laslui Lake, near the headwaters of the Stikine River. The wooden tombstone read, simply, "Love Old Man Antoine died 1926." Curious about the grave, I crossed the lake to the mouth of Hotleskwa Creek, where the Collingwood brothers, the outfitters for the Spatsizi, had established a spike camp. There I found Alex Jack, an old Gitksan man who had lived in the mountains most of his life. His native name was Atehena, "he who walks leaving no tracks." Not only did Alex know of the grave, his own brother-in-law had laid the body to rest in it. Old Man Antoine, it turned out, was a legendary shaman, crippled from birth but possessed of the gift of clairvoyance. Alex had walked overland from his home at Bear Lake in the Skeena, 150 miles to the south, in order to meet Antoine, only to arrive on the day of his death.

Intrigued by this link between a living elder, raised in seasonally nomadic encampments, totally dependent on the hunt, and a shaman born in the previous century who read the future in stones cast into water held in baskets woven from roots, I left my job as a park ranger and went to work with Alex. As we wrangled horses, repaired fences, guided the odd hunter in search of moose or goat, I would ask him to tell me the stories of the old days, the myths of his people and his land. He happily told tales of his youth, of the hunting forays that had brought meat to the village and of the winter trading runs by dogsled to the coast, but he never said a word about the legends.

Long after I had given up on hearing the origin myths, I went out one morning to salvage a moose carcass abandoned by a trophy hunter. When I returned after a long day with a canoe full of meat, Alex was waiting for me. As we walked back across the meadow with our loads, he said very quietly that he remembered a story and invited me to drop by his tent later in the evening. To this day I do not know whether I had achieved a certain level of trust with Alex, or whether I had finally inquired about the stories in the correct manner, or whether the gift of meat had some greater significance. But that night I began to record a long series of creator tales of We-gyet, the anthropomorphic figure of folly, the trickster/transformer of Gitksan lore.

They were almost all whimsical stories of moral gratitude played out against and within the backdrop of nature. We-gyet, for example, eager to eat, swims beneath a gathering of swans and greedily grabs their legs, only to be dragged from the water as the flock rises in response, soaring toward the sun. Stranded in the sky, he lets go and comes crashing back to the Earth, the force of the impact imbedding him in granite. A lynx comes by, and We-gyet, using his charm and guile, persuades the cat to lick away the rock. We-gyet rewards his savior with the tufts of hair that have since that time decorated the ears of every lynx.

To kill a grizzly, We-gyet takes advantage of the creature's pride. Moving with the speed of the wind, he flies past a berry patch, astonishing the bear with his grace and movements. The grizzly looks up, only to see We-gyet race by once more. After three passes, We-gyet stops, breathlessly approaches his prey, and collapses with laughter as he points disparagingly at the bear's testicles. "No wonder you can't run," he comments, "with those things dangling between your legs. I cut mine off years ago. See?" We-gyet has stained his groin with the blood-red sap of a willow. The grizzly, eager to remain the dominant creature in the forest, slices off his genitals and promptly bleeds to death.

Animals large and small featured in Alex's tales. A hunting party away from home for many days grows tired, the young boys restless and bored. To pass the time, they cast a squirrel into their fire, a cruel act repeated again and again until the creature, unable to escape, disappears in the flames. The following morning, the hunters awake to find themselves camped in a circle at the base of an enormous cylinder of rock that reaches to the heavens, bluffs on all sides, no escape. Perplexed, a warrior tosses a pack dog into the fire, and to his surprise the animal appears at the top of the rock face. One by one, each hunter slips into the flames and materializes alongside the dog, thus miraculously escaping the trap. They head for home, but when they enter their village and approach their loved ones, no one sees them. They reach out and try to touch their wives and mothers. Their hands pass through the bodies like air. They are all dead, ghosts empty of will, punished for the crime of having, as Alex put it, "suffered that small squirrel."

Darkness is the time for stories, and in the glow of a kerosene lamp, with wind and rain falling upon the canvas, the tent that first night took on the warmth of a womb. Alex's words themselves had a certain magic, a power to influence not only the listener but the land itself. When he told a story, he did not, as we might, recount an anecdote, which by definition is a literary device, an abstraction, the condensation of a memory extracted from the stream of experience, a recollection of facts strung together with words. Alex actually lived the story again and again, returning in body and soul, in physical gesture and nuance, to the very place and time of its origin. At first I thought this merely charming, and only after many years of listening, often to the same account told in the same way time and again, did I understand the significance of what he was sharing.

Alex did not come from a tradition of literacy. He had never learned to read or write with any degree of fluency. For most of his adult life, he had been a seasonally nomadic hunter; his very vocabulary was inspired by the sounds of the wild. For him, the sweeping flight of a hawk was the cursive hand of nature, a script written on the wind. As surely as we can hear the voices of characters as we read the pages of a novel, so Alex could hear in his mind the voices of animals, creatures that he both revered and hunted. Their meat kept him alive. Their skins could be worked into leather for moccasins and clothes, packsacks and the traces of his sled, the scabbard for his 30.06 rifle. Their blood could be cooked, the marrow of their bones sucked out and fed as a delicacy to children.

When Alex told a story, he did so in such a way that the listener actually witnessed and experienced the essence of the tale, entering the narrative and becoming transfixed by all the syllables of nature. Every telling was a moment of renewal, a chance to engage through repetition in the circular dance of the universe.

Alex never spoke ill of the wind or the cold. When hunting, he never referred to the prey by name until after the kill; then he spoke directly to the animal with praise and respect, admiring its strength and cleverness. His grandmother was Cree, people of the medicine power, who believe that language was given to humans by the animals. His mother was Carrier. In 1924, two years before Alex left Bear Lake to walk overland to the Stikine, an elder from the Bulkley Valley, quite possibly one of Alex's relatives, revealed something of the Carrier world to the anthropologist Diamond Jenness:

> *We know what the animals do, what are the needs of the beaver, the bear, the salmon and other creatures, because long ago men married them and*

acquired this knowledge from their animal wives. Today the priests say we lie, but we know better. The white man has only been a short while in this country and knows very little about the animals; we have lived here thousands of years and were taught by the animals themselves. The white man writes everything down in a book so that it will not be forgotten; but our ancestors married animals, learned all their ways, and passed on this knowledge from one generation to another.

I did indeed write down Alex's tales, transcriptions of dozens of hours of conversations recorded intermittently over 25 years, committed to paper a few years before his death. Only after I finished did I realize that in a sense I had committed a form of violence, a transgression that bordered on betrayal. Extracted from the theater of his telling, the landscape of his memory, the sensate land, and the sibilant tones of the wild, the stories lost much of their meaning and power. Transposed into two dimensions by ink and paper, trapped on the page, they seemed childlike in their simplicity, even clumsy in their rhetoric.

But, of course, these stories were not meant to be recorded. They were born of the land and had their origins in another reality. Some time after I first learned of We-gyet from Alex, I asked him how long it took to tell the cycle of tales. He replied that he had asked his father that very question. To find out, they had strapped on their snowshoes in March, a time of good ice, and walked the length of Bear Lake, a distance of 20 miles, telling the story as they went along. They reached the far end, turned, and walked all the way back home, and the story, Alex recalled, "wasn't halfway done."

In order to measure the duration of a story, the length of a myth, it was not enough to set a timepiece. One had to move through geography, telling the tale as one proceeded. For Alex and his father, this sense of place, this topography of the spirit, at one time informed every aspect of their existence. When at the turn of the century a Catholic missionary arrived at their village at Bear Lake, Alex's father was completely confounded by the Christian notion of heaven. He could not believe that anyone could be expected to give up smoking, gambling, swearing, carousing, and all the things that made life worth living in order to go to a place where they did not allow animals. "No caribou?" he would say in complete astonishment. He could not conceive of a world without wild things.

Alex lived for more than 90 years; his wife Madeleine reached 103, passing away a few seasons before Alex followed her to the grave. A year before he died, Alex gave me a small gift, a tool carved from caribou bone. Smooth as marble, though stained from years of use, it fit perfectly in my hand, the rounded and slightly serrated spoon-like tip protruding neatly from between finger and thumb. I had no idea what it might have been used for. Alex laughed. He had carved it more than 80 years before, following the lead of his father. It was a specialized instrument, used to skin out the eyelids of wolves. Only later did I realize that the eyelids in question were my own, and that Alex, having done so much to allow me to see, was, in his own way, saying good-bye.

＊

A YEAR OR TWO AFTER ALEX PASSED AWAY, I found myself one afternoon in the small Andean town of Chincheros just outside of Cuzco, sitting on a rock throne carved from granite. At my back was the sacred mountain Antakillqa, lost in dark clouds yet illuminated in a mysterious way by a rainbow that arched across its flank. Below me, the terraces of Chincheros fell away to an emerald plain, the floor of an ancient seabed, beyond which rose the ridges of the distant Vilcabamba, the last redoubt of the Inca, a landscape of holy shrines and lost dreams where Tupac Amarú waged war and the spirit of the Sun still ruled for 50 years after the Conquest. Two young boys played soccer on the village green, a plaza where once Topa Inca Yupanqui, second of the great Inca rulers, reviewed his troops. On the very stone where I rested, he no doubt had stood; this village of adobe and whitewashed homes, this warren of cobblestones, mud, and grass, had been built upon the ruins of his summer palace.

For 400 years the Catholic Church, perched at the height of the ruins overlooking the market square, had dominated the site. A beautiful sanctuary, it bears today none of the scars of the Conquest. It is a place of worship that belongs to the people, and there are no echoes of tyranny. Within its soaring vault, in a space illuminated by candles and the light of pale Andean skies, I once stood at the altar a newborn child in my arms, a boy swaddled in white linen. An itinerant priest dripped holy water onto his forehead and spoke words of blessing that brought the infant into the realm of the saved. After the baptism there was a celebration, and the child's parents, my new compadres, toasted every hopeful possibility. I too made promises, which in the ensuing years I attempted to fulfill. I had no illusions about the economic foundation of the bond. From me, my compadres hoped to secure support: in time, money for my godchild's education, perhaps the odd gift, a cow for the family, a measure of security in an uncertain nation. From them I wanted nothing but the chance to know their world, an asset far more valuable than anything I could offer.

This pact, never spoken about and never forgotten, was in its own way a perfect reflection of the Andes, where the foundation of all life, both today and in the time of the Inca, has always been reciprocity. One sees it in the fields, when men come together and work in teams, moving between rows of fava beans and potatoes, season to season, a day for a day, planting, hoeing, weeding, mounding, harvesting. There is a spiritual exchange in the morning when the first of a family to awake salutes the sun, and again at night when a father whispers prayers of thanksgiving and lights a candle before greeting his family. Every offering is a gift: blossoms scattered onto fertile fields, the blessing of the children and tools at the end of each day, coca leaves presented to Pachamama at any given moment. When people meet on a trail, they pause and exchange *k'intu*s of coca, three perfect leaves aligned to form a cross. Turning to face the nearest *apu*, or mountain spirit, they bring the leaves to the mouth and blow softly, a ritual invocation that sends the essence of the plant back to the earth, the community, the sacred places, and the souls of the ancestors. The exchange of leaves is a social gesture, a way of acknowledging a human connection. But the blowing of the *phukuy*, as it is called, is an act of spiritual reciprocity. In giving selflessly to the earth, the individual ensures that in time the energy of the coca will return full circle, as surely as rain falling on a field will inevitably be reborn as a cloud.

Almost 20 years after first visiting Chincheros, I returned to participate in an astonishing ritual, the *mujonimiento*, the annual running of the boundaries. Since the time of the Inca, the town has been divided into three *ayullus*, or communities, the most traditional of which is Cuper, the home of my compadres and, to my mind, the most beautiful, for its lands encompass Antakillqa and all the soaring ridges that separate Chincheros from the sacred valley of the Urubamba. Within Cuper are four hamlets, and once each year, at the height of the rainy season, the entire male population, save those elders physically incapable of the feat, runs the boundaries of their respective communities. It is a race but also a pilgrimage, for the frontiers are marked by mounds of earth, holy sites where prayers are uttered and ritual gestures lay claim to the land. The distance traveled by the members of each hamlet varies. The track I was to follow, that of Pucamarca, covers 15 miles, but the route crosses two Andean ridges, dropping a thousand feet from the plaza of Chincheros to the base of Antakillqa, then ascending 3,000 feet to a summit spur before descending to the valley on the far side, only to climb once more to reach the grasslands of the high puna and the long trail home.

At the head of each contingent would dart the *waylaka*, the strongest and fleetest of the youths, transformed for the day from male to female. Dressed in heavy woolen skirts and a cloak of indigo, wearing a woman's hat and delicate lace, the waylaka would fly up the ridges, white banner in hand. At every boundary marker the transvestite must dance, a rhythmic turn that like a vortex draws to the peaks the energy of the women left behind in the villages far below. Each of the four hamlets of Cuper has its own trajectory, just as each of the three ayullus has its own land to traverse. By the end of the day, all of Chincheros would be reclaimed: the rich plains and verdant fields of Ayullupunqu; the lakes, waterfalls, mountains, and cliffs of Cuper; the gorges of Yanacona, where wild things thrive and rushing streams carry away the rains to the Urubamba. Adversaries would have been fought, spirits invoked, a landscape defined, and the future secured.

This much I knew as I approached the plaza on the morning of the event. Before dawn, the blowing of the conch shells had awoken the town, and the waylakas, once dressed, had walked from house to house saluting the various authorities: the *curaca* and alcalde; the officers of the church; and the *embarados*, those charged with the preservation of tradition. At each threshold, coca had been exchanged, fermented maize *chicha* imbibed, and a cross of flowers hung in reverence above the doorway. For two hours the procession had moved from door to door, musicians in tow, until it encompassed all of the community and drew everyone in celebration to the plaza, where women waited, food in hand: baskets of potatoes and spicy *piquante*, flasks of chicha, and steaming plates of vegetables. There I lingered, with gifts of coca for all. At my side was my godson, Armando. A grown man now, father of an infant girl, he had been a tailor but worked now in the markets of Cuzco, delivering sacks of potatoes on a tricycle rented from a cousin. He had returned to Chincheros to be with me for the day.

What I could never have anticipated was the excitement and the rush of adrenaline, the sensation of imminent flight as the entire assembly of men, prompted by some unspoken signal, began to surge toward the end of the plaza. With a shout, the waylaka sprang down through the ruins, carrying with him more than a hundred runners and dozens of young boys who scattered across the slopes that funneled downward toward a narrow dirt track. The trail fell away through a copse of eucalyptus and passed along the banks of a creek that dropped to the valley floor. A mile or two on, the waylaka paused for an instant, took measure of the men, caught his breath, and was off, dashing through thickets of buddleia and polylepis as the rest of us scrambled to keep sight of his white banner. Crossing the creek draw, we moved up the face of Antakillqa. Here at last the pace slowed to something less than a full run. Still, the men leaned into the slope with an intensity and determination unlike anything I had ever known. Less than two hours after leaving the village, we reached the summit ridge, a climb of several thousand feet.

There we paused, as the waylaka planted his banner atop a *mujon*, a tall mound of dirt, the first of the border markers. The authorities added their ceremonial staffs, and as the men piled on dirt to augment the size of the mujon, Don Jeronimo, the curaca, sang rich invocations that broke into a cheer for the well-being of the entire community. By this point the runners were as restless as racehorses, frantic to move. A salutation, a prayer, a generous farewell to those of Cuper Pueblo (another of the hamlets) who would track north, and we of Pucamarca were off, heading east across the back side of the mountain to a second mujon located on a dramatic promontory overlooking all of the Urubamba. Beyond the hamlets and farms of the sacred valley, clouds swirled across the flanks of even higher mountains as great shafts of sunlight fell upon the river and the fields far below.

We pounded on across the back side of the mountain and then straight down at a full run through dense tufts of *ichu* grass and meadows of lupine and rue. Another mujon, more prayers, hand-fuls of coca all around, blessings and shouts, and a mad dash off the mountain to the valley floor, where, mercifully, we older men rested for a few minutes in the courtyard of a farmstead owned by a beautiful elderly woman who greeted us with a great ceramic urn of frothy chicha. One of the authorities withdrew from his pocket a sheet of paper listing the names of the men and began to take attendance. Participation in the mujonimiento is obligatory, and those who fail to appear must pay a fine to the community. As the names were called, I glanced up and was stunned to see the way-laka, silhouetted on the skyline hundreds of feet above us, banner in hand, moving on.

So the day went. The rains began in early afternoon and the winds blew fiercely by four. By then nothing mattered but the energy of the group, the trail at our feet, and the distant slope of yet another ridge to climb. Warmed by alcohol and coca leaves, the runners fell into reverie, a curious state of joy and release, almost like a trance.

Darkness was upon us as we rushed down the final canyon on a broad muddy track where the water ran together like mercury and disappeared beneath the stones. Approaching the valley floor and the hamlet of Cuper Alto, where women and children waited, the rain-soaked runners closed ranks behind the waylaka to emerge from the mountains as a single force, an entire community that had affirmed through ritual its sense of place and belonging. In making the sacrifice, the men had reclaimed a birthright and rendered sacred a homeland. Once reunited with their families, they drank and sang, toasting their good fortune as the women served great steaming bowls of soup from iron cauldrons. And, of course, late into the night the waylakas danced.

＊

BOTH OF THESE ACCOUNTS REVEAL the role that ritual plays in forging the bonds of memory that define a people's sense of place and belonging. Each indicates as well the importance of embracing metaphor as we attempt to understand traditional relationships to land, history, community, and the spirit realm. Ultimately, this is our great challenge. How do we, who have grown so distant from the soil and the mystic threads of recollection that gave rise to our being, explain the wonder of those peoples who still engage the land? Most of our popular explanations come up short. Many still invoke Rousseau, implying that indigenous peoples are somehow by nature closer to the land than we can possibly be, an idea not only silly, but racist in its simplicity. Others recall Thoreau, as if to suggest that indigenous peoples are more conscious and contemplative about their place in nature than those of us born into the industrial world.

Indigenous peoples, in truth, are neither sentimental nor weakened by nostalgia. Life in the malarial swamps of New Guinea, the chill winds of Tibet, the white heat of the Sahara, leaves little room for sentiment. Nostalgia is not a trait commonly associated with the Inuit. Nomadic hunters and gatherers in Borneo have no conscious sense of stewardship for mountain forests that they lack the technical capacity to destroy. What these cultures have done, however, is to forge through time and ritual a traditional mystique of the Earth that is based not only on deep attachment to the land but also on far more subtle intuition—the idea that the land itself is breathed into being by human consciousness. Mountains, rivers, and forests are not perceived as inanimate, as mere props on a stage upon which the human drama unfolds. For these societies the land is alive, a dynamic force to be embraced and transformed by the human imagination. Here lies the essence of the relationship between indigenous peoples and the natural world.

Around ten thousand years ago, the Neolithic revolution transformed human destiny; with agriculture came surplus, specialization, hierarchy, and a religious worldview that displaced the poetry of the shaman with the prose of the institutional priesthood. Three hundred years ago at the dawn of the industrial age, the spirit of the Enlightenment liberated the individual from the constraints of community. This was an even more profound innovation, the sociological equivalent of the splitting of the atom. Still, in much of the world, neither innovation took hold. In Australia, the Aboriginal peoples neither freed the individual nor succumbed to the cult of progress. For thousands of years they traveled lightly on the land. To be sure, they set fire to grasslands and forest, killed what game they could. But for the most part, their impact on their environment was nominal. Why did this happen? Why were they exempt from the impulses to improve on the wild that propelled our ancestors? An explanation may be found in the fundamental beliefs and convictions that defined their existence.

The Europeans who colonized Australia were unprepared for the sophistication of the place and its inhabitants, incapable of embracing its wonder. They had no understanding of the challenges of the desert and little sensitivity to the achievements of Aboriginal peoples who for over 60,000 years had thrived as nomads, wanderers on a pristine continent. In all that time the desire to improve upon the natural world, to tame the rhythm of the wild, had never touched them. The Aborigines accepted life as it was, a cosmological whole, the unchanging creation of the first dawn, when earth and sky separated and the original Ancestor brought into being all the primordial Ancestors who, through their thoughts, dreams, and journeys, sang the world into existence.

The Ancestors walked as they sang, and when it was time to stop, they slept. In their dreams they conceived the events of the following day, points of creation that fused one into another until every creature, every stream and stone, all time and space, became part of the whole, the divine manifestation of the one great seminal impulse. When they grew exhausted from their labors, they retired into the earth, sky, clouds, rivers, lakes, plants, and animals of an island continent that resonates with their memory. The paths taken by the Ancestors have never been forgotten. They are the Songlines, precise itineraries followed even today as the people travel across the template of the physical world.

As the Aborigines track the Songlines and chant the stories of the first dawning, they become part of the Ancestors and enter the Dreamtime, which is neither a dream nor a measure of the passage of time. It is the very realm of the Ancestors, a parallel universe where the ordinary laws of time, space, and motion do not apply, where past, future, and present merge into one. It is a place that Europeans can approximate only in sleep, and thus it became known to the early English settlers as the Dreaming, or Dreamtime. But the term is misleading. A dream by Western definition is a state of consciousness divorced from the real world. The Dreamtime, by contrast, is the real world, or at least one of two realities experienced in the daily lives of the Aborigines.

To walk the Songlines is to become part of the ongoing creation of the world, a place that both exists and is still being formed. Thus, the Aborigines are not merely attached to the earth; they are essential to its existence. Without the land, they would die. But without the people, the ongoing process of creation would cease and the Earth would wither. Through movement and sacred rituals, the people maintain access to the Dreamtime and play a dynamic and ongoing role in the world of the Ancestors.

A moment begins with nothing. A man or a woman walks, and from emptiness emerge the songs, the musical embodiment of reality, the cosmic melodies that give the world its character. The songs create vibrations that take shape. Dancing brings definition to the forms, and objects of the phenomenological realm appear: trees, rocks, streams, all of them physical evidence of the Dreaming. Should the rituals stop, the voices fall silent, all would be lost—everything on Earth is held together by the Songlines, everything is subordinate to the Dreaming, which is constant but ever changing. Every landmark is wedded to a memory of its origins and yet always being born. Every animal and object resonates with the pulse of an ancient event, while still being dreamed into being. The world as it exists is perfect, though constantly in the process of being formed. The land is encoded with everything that ever has been and everything that ever will be in every dimension of reality. To walk the land is to engage in a constant act of affirmation, an endless dance of creation.

The Europeans who first washed ashore on the beaches of Australia lacked the language or imagination even to begin to understand the profound intellectual and spiritual achievements of the Aborigines. What they saw was a people who lived simply, whose technological achievements were modest, whose faces looked strange, whose habits were incomprehensible. The Aborigines lacked all the hallmarks of European civilization. They had no metal tools, knew nothing of writing, had never succumbed to the cult of the seed. Without agriculture or animal husbandry, they generated no surpluses, and thus had never embraced sedentary village life. Hierarchy and specialization were unknown. Their small seminomadic bands living in temporary shelters made of sticks and grass, dependent on stone weapons, epitomized European notions of backwardness. An early French explorer described them as "the most miserable people of the world, human beings who approach closest to brute beasts." As late as 1902, a member of the Australian Parliament claimed, "There is no scientific evidence that the Aborigine is a human at all."

By the 1930s, a combination of disease, exploitation, and murder had reduced the Aborigine population from well over a million at the time of European contact to less than half a million. In one century a land bound together by Songlines, where the people moved effortlessly from one dimension to the next, from the future to the past and from the past to the present, was transformed from Eden to Armageddon. Knowing what we do today of the extraordinary reach of the Aboriginal mind, the subtlety of their thoughts, and the evocative power of their rituals, it is chilling to think this reservoir of human potential, wisdom, intuition, and insight very nearly ran dry during those terrible years of death and conflagration. As it is, Aboriginal languages, which may have numbered 250 at the time of contact, are disappearing at the rate of one or more per year. Only 18 are today spoken by 500 or more individuals.

Despite this history, the Aborigines have survived and, in time, may still have a chance to inspire and redeem a nation. But what of the other victims of conquest, the untold scores of nations driven out of existence by forces beyond their capacity to engage and overcome?

✳

FOR AT LEAST 10,000 YEARS the San Bushman occupied the sandveld regions of Botswana, Namibia, and southern Angola. Numbering perhaps 85,000, they were the descendants of a people who inhabited the entire subcontinent and much of East Africa thousands of years before the arrival of either black or white pastoralists and farmers. Unlike the agriculturists, who spread inexorably across the land, transforming the wild and constantly moving onward, the nomadic San essentially stayed put, engaged as hunters and gatherers in a seasonal round that left little mark on the Earth. Like the Aboriginal peoples of Australia, they accepted the world as it was, and rather than struggle with the natural world, they moved to its rhythm—not out of conviction, but because their survival depended upon doing so. Thus they adapted to what was without doubt one of the most extreme landscapes on the planet.

Water is the great challenge. For ten months of the year there is none, at least on the surface of the ground. The San traditionally sought moisture in the hollows of trees, used hollow reeds to suck it out of sipwells beneath the mud, or resorted to hidden supplies, cached in ostrich eggs buried beneath the sand and marked with the insignia of the owner. For most of the year there was no water at all and the people were totally dependent on melons and tubers, and whatever liquid could be squeezed from the guts of prey. To replenish the three quarts of moisture lost each day through perspiration, the San had to consume 12 pounds of wild melon. And with the onset of the dry season in May, the melons shriveled, and the people were forced to dig for tubers deep within the sand. Throughout the year plants provided 80 percent of their food, but 90 percent of their water. The possibility of dying of thirst was a constant.

By September, the season of the Brown Hyena, the time of greatest privation, the San spent their days lying still in shallow hollows moistened with urine, tormented by clouds of flies and tortured by the withering heat. October marked the beginning of the Little Rains, teasing raindrops that touch the Earth but do little to relieve the drought. The heat continues. High winds sweep over the burned grasslands, and the spirits of the dead appear in the shape of dust devils, dancing across a gray and yellow landscape. Finally in January the rains return, and the next three months are a time of rebirth and regeneration. Some years great rolling clouds break open to flood the desert with thunderous downpours, inches of precious water that form silver sheets upon the desert. Some years it does not rain at all.

The rainy season from January to March is a time of relative abundance. People move about the desert in small extended family groups, harvesting seeds and fruit, rejoicing to find standing pools of water or hives of bees with rare offerings of honey, a sublime delicacy for a people whose diet for much of the year consists of fibrous roots and bitter tubers. April brings yet another change, a short autumn, the season of the hunter. This for the San is the favorite time of year. The rains have driven away the heat and the cold of winter has yet to descend. There is ripe food everywhere and the animals are fat.

Though the San depend largely on plants for their food, it is the act of hunting that defines them as a people. From family encampments the men range across the desert in small hunting parties of three or four, covering as much as 20 miles in a day, returning by night only to hunt again with the dawn. They carry just their weapons and a few essentials, a short bow and quiver of arrows, fire-making tools, a hollow reed to sip water from the sand, perhaps a knife, a short spear, a lump of gum or resin to make repairs. Moving in teams, they read the ground for signs. Nothing is overlooked. A trodden blade of grass, the direction of a tear in a leaf, the depth and shape of a track. Legendary stalkers, the San can distinguish and follow the sign of a single wounded animal though it moves in a herd of thousands. Every human footprint has a name, for the San recognize a person's mark with the precision of a forensic expert linking a fingerprint to a suspect.

Everything is hunted. Hippos die in pits lined with poisoned poles. Elephants are brought down with the blow of an ax to the hamstring. Lions sluggish from gorging on meat are chased from a kill. Antelope are run to the ground, birds snared in nets woven from desert fibers. The hunting gear is primitive—spears and small arrows of limited range. But for the San the key to success as hunters lies in their knowledge of the prey and of the plants and beetle grubs, which properly prepared yield the most lethal of poisons. The slightest wound results in convulsions, paralysis, and death.

From the desert adaptation emerges a way of life. Nothing is wasted, least of all one's own energy. In the heat of midday, people remain still. Taboos reserve certain foods for the weak and elderly: tortoise and ostrich eggs and other creatures such as snakes readily found and killed. All food is shared. To refuse a gift is an act of unforgivable hostility. To accept is to acknowledge one's place in a community of life.

For the San, who never stay long in one place and yet never travel far from the land of their birth, the center of social life is the encampment and the sacred fire that burns at its heart. For these desert peoples, the sun is not a sign of life, but a symbol of death. Life is found in the family hearth, the fire that brings warmth in the night and provides shelter in the darkness. A mother gives birth in the shadows and returns to the fire. When a marriage fails, a young girl slips away and heads home to her father's fire. An elder, no longer capable of keeping up with his group, is left behind to die, a circle of brush built around him to keep back the hyenas, a fire at his feet to lead him on to the next world. To placate the God of the West, the spirits of the dead, and all the forces of evil, the San dance, spinning around the fire in trance, placing their heads in the burning coals as the energy moves up their spines, touching the base of their skulls and diffusing through their bodies and into the earth itself. Whenever trouble threatens, the San kindle a fire and find solace and protection in the flames.

Pack horses above Lake Louise, Canadian Rockies, Alberta PIERRE LEMIRE

ecological integrity   ✳   SID MARTY

Each mountain its own country
In the way a country must be
A state of mind

SID MARTY, "EACH MOUNTAIN"

BANFF NATIONAL PARK began as a 10-square-mile reserve surrounding the hot springs on Sulphur Mountain in 1885. Canada's first park was eventually expanded to include 2,564 square miles (6,641 square kilometers) of Rocky Mountain terrain, much of it standing on end as rocky peaks and glaciated mountains, ranging in altitude from 8,000 feet on its eastern slopes to more than 11,000 feet on the Continental Divide. Today, Banff is part of a mountain ecosystem that includes the neighboring Yoho, Kootenay, and Jasper National Parks, some of the most scenic landscapes on Earth. Banff is the best known of Canada's 39 national parks, and perhaps the most seriously threatened by human uses. Four and a half million visitors enter the park every year, and thousands of them come from abroad—especially from Great Britain, Germany, and Japan.

As a park warden from 1966 to 1978 and for six months in 1988, I worked in both Yoho and Jasper parks and spent the last years of my career in the grizzly country of Banff Park, on foot and on horseback, chasing the seasons. So I came to know firsthand this vital remnant of the Canadian wilderness, most of which vanished from southern Canada by 1900. The warden service was, and still is, the backbone of the national parks—their heart and soul.

In that mountain outfit we took our share of scars and broken bones. We tracked the wounded down, dispatching big game animals crippled by trucks and trains on the "Meatmakers," also known as the Trans-Canada Highway and the Canadian Pacific Railway. Late in the fall we were out "pushing the boundary" on horseback patrols, prowling the passes, oftentimes alone, watching for poachers. We took our chances at mountain rescue work; we saved some lives and recovered the remains of others. We fished those who drowned from the rivers and dug human statues out of avalanches. We paid our dues. So it should be no surprise that my heart sank watching the environmental degradation of the Bow Valley in Banff Park. Watching the fierce light go out in the eyes of grizzly bears that brooked no compromise with men, I saw how we'd broken our promise to give them a sanctuary. In truth, such a lofty land deserves scores of wardens, and right now, it needs millions of defenders.

Some think of mountains as extreme landscapes. I've always thought of them as sublime. It is a definition I think that fits many landscapes, including the Arctic tundra, the great deserts, the Himalaya, and the upper reaches of the European Alps, to name a few. A step into Canada's sublime landscapes is often a step back in time, a reconsideration that begins with a revelation— "So this is what it was like;—was it really only a century ago?" But at that moment a jetliner's contrail high overhead shapes a question mark one cannot ignore: Is this roadless cordillera just a living museum of what once was, or is it truly wild?

I would say yes, there is still some true wilderness here, and I believe, as Henry David Thoreau and John Muir and James Bernard Harkin (esteemed parks commissioner) did, that in wilderness lies the hope of the world. But this wilderness is subject to the same kind of threats caused by climatic changes and air pollution that are found elsewhere on Earth. And the national park back country exists by an act of human will. Its internal integrity is not assured, and it is threatened on its periphery by creeping resource extraction, roads, and subdivisions, which have made its remote reaches simply wilderness islands in a crowded human sea. This threatens the survival of wildlife like mountain goats, bighorn sheep, grizzly bears, and wolves. The last two need hundreds of square miles to survive. Beasts cannot read maps, and when they step across the magic line onto provincial land, they all too often step in front of a hunter's gun.

As a result of my adventures in practical conservation— conservation that works in practice rather than in theory—I can't conceive of landscapes divorced from their ecological content, as mere obstacles to be "summited." One of the most hopeful documents Parks Canada ever commissioned, and the key to its own transformation and renewal, is the "Report of the Panel on the Ecological Integrity of Canada's National Parks" (published in 2000): "In plain language," the EI Report reads, "ecosystems have integrity when they have their native components (plants, animals, and other organisms) and processes (such as growth and reproduction) intact." In my opinion, a landscape is degraded, it loses a part of the sublime quality we value, when its ecological integrity is threatened, even when the changes are too subtle to be apparent. Plants, animals, and human beings too, when the latter are living in balance with the land, are part of the sublime landscape.

Mountains, animated every moment by light and shadow, given voice by the wind's quarrel with gendarmes of rock and by the hunting songs of gray wolves, girdled by spruce, garlanded by a necklace of golden larches every fall, source of water that sustains the prairie earth and everything that moves upon it: Could these be mere objects? We must be mad indeed if we think a mountain is not alive. It is this notion, I believe, not their altitude, their severity, their punishing weather and relentless objectivity, that teaches us to approach them with humility.

Mountain earth is mainly stone; its thin green skin, the tentative kiss of life on bedrock, is easily scarred. A mountain can be wounded, and the human race, whose actions taken cumulatively are now viewed by some scientists as an actual agent of geographic change, can do the wounding in a startling variety of ways. Our effluents are a global miasma that feeds on ozone. The forest fires that raged out of control at unprecedented levels last year, the droughts that congealed the east slope streams of Alberta and shrank well water, or the permafrost melting in the Arctic are just recent reminders that it is long past time for action on the Kyoto Accords.

Mount Everest has been degraded by human excesses and the Canadian Rockies are not immune. That snowy crown, the Victoria Glacier at Lake Louise, marks the birthplace of mountaineering in Canada and epitomizes the Canadian Rockies in photos published all over the world. It was designated a United Nations world heritage site in 1985. But due to global warming, this masterpiece of the Maker's hand has declined drastically since I first climbed its peaks a mere 40 years ago. The glaciated Abbot Pass, between Mounts Victoria and Lefroy, was a rite of passage for any beginning alpinist. Now the ice is stretched thin, fractured into a dangerous warren of cracks and seracs, posing extreme hazards to climbers. It is a grim testament to the power of man-made pollutants and global warming.

More dangerous changes have recently come to light. The residues of chemical agriculture may now threaten global watersheds. As famed water ecologist David Schindler has pointed out, the rapid melting of some Alberta glaciers has released persistent organic pollutants like PCB, DDT, and other poisons, which were deposited on the ice as airborne toxins two decades ago. Where they originated is not clear. When heated by the sun, these toxins vaporize and are carried great distances by air currents—the grasshopper effect—only to be precipitated over cooler zones far from where they were first distributed. They are now filtering into drinking water. They flow into rivers; they are collected as poisons in tiny alpine lakes; they accumulate in the food chain from mollusk to cutthroat trout to man. The higher up the mountains, the greater the concentration of these toxins. They are bio-magnifiers that lodge in human tissues and interfere with endocrine and reproductive glands. Scientists suspect that glaciers throughout the world, the source of 70 percent of drinking water, will prove to be equally contaminated once tests are done. It is a bitter reflection to think of all the poisoned water I drank in mountain wanderings, while thinking it was the purest water the sun could make. What does it mean for our future health? When we come to the defense of glaciated landscapes, we are defending more than aesthetic principles; we are defending our lives. So even in these extreme landscapes human-influenced climatic and geophysical forces are at work, altering their beauty, shrinking and poisoning their waters.

Machine man lives in a world of noise, all hum, twang, rap and ecstatic. The lack of this white noise leaves your head ringing for a while after you enter the stillness of the bush. And this anvil chorus, ever increasing, signals your return. When you step out from behind the pine tree curtain into the Bow Valley in Banff Park, the song is playing fortissimo. It's the bass roar of transport trucks, the percussive rumble of trains, 30 of them each day rolling down the nation's first railroad.

The wilderness ideal we now take for granted, the notion that wilderness experience is an egalitarian social good, was novel to North Americans at the founding of Yellowstone National Park in 1872. But the news has spread worldwide to 1,200 parks in 100 countries since then. Cornelius Hedges, a Yellowstone advocate of the 1870s, expressed it thus: "This great wilderness does not belong to us. It belongs to the nation. Let us make a public park of it, and set it aside...never to be changed but to be kept sacred always." Still, Americans were slow in exploring their first park; it was beset for years with road agents, buffalo skinners, and fugitive Bannock and Nez Perce warriors until the Army moved in to protect it in 1885.

What made Canada's first park possible was the need of the Canadian Pacific Railway (CPR) to attract wealthy passengers whose fares would help pay for that mammoth national undertaking. In 1885, few Canadians saw the need to keep wilderness sacred. The underpopulated country, its frigid homes still heated by wood and coal, was one wilderness from coast to coast. The country needed roads, bridges, markets, and commerce. The medicinal waters of Banff's hot springs were regarded as a resource to be exploited. The parliamentary act that gave birth to the first park described it in homely terms as "a national park and sanatorium." But other advocates of the park did not share Hedges's egalitarian views. William Cornelius Van Horne, president of the CPR, summed up the tenor of the times in a sentence: "These springs are worth a million dollars!" He meant for the CPR, of course. He would promote the Rockies as the Canadian Pacific Rockies and build grand hotels, such as the Banff Springs, to capture the tourist trade. His attitude set the tone for CPR operations in the mountains for decades.

Another advocate, Prime Minister Sir John A. Macdonald, had helped tie the nation together with steel rails from ocean to ocean. Now he became the first park subdivider, ordering villa lots at Banff to be plotted and then "leased out to wealthy people." He assured parliament that "the doubtful class of people," meaning poorer Canadians, would not be welcome in the new resort. He approved expenditures to "make the park useful" with carriage roads, bathhouses, and picnic grounds. From the start, he insisted the park must generate revenues and "recoup the treasury." His parks act did, however, provide a few key clauses for the preservation and protection of the landscape and the wildlife.

John Muir's transcendentalist muse made few inroads in park management until James Bernard Harkin was appointed commissioner of what was then known as the Dominion Parks Branch in 1911. "The parks belong to the people," said Harkin, and under his purview, citizens were made welcome, aided by that great democratic leveler—the automobile—and the number of parks rapidly increased. He fought hard to protect wildlife and remove logging and mining interests. But the need to "recoup the treasury" caught Harkin up in a vicious circle. Increased tourism demanded more and more development (swimming pools and highways), which demanded more funding, which in turn demanded more visitation. He came to realize that "Use without abuse" would be the central problem of the future, and so he framed a clause in the 1930 National Parks Act that has haunted environmentalists ever since: "The parks are hereby dedicated to the people of Canada for their benefit, education and enjoyment...and such parks shall be maintained and made use of so as to leave them unimpaired for the enjoyment of future generations."

Over the decades, Banff tried to be all things to all people. Park managers talked about the dual mandate, but few senior managers were true conservationists of Harkin's stamp. What they focused on was the public's right for use and enjoyment—not impairment—of park landscapes and natural cycles.

Wildlife have paid a heavy price. Only one percent of Banff Park is heavily developed, but 37 percent of the park consists of inhospitable rock and ice. Of the land remaining, only 3 percent, the montane valley habitat, is rich enough to sustain wintering range for the park's elk herd. But this same habitat is most desirable for human use. The townsites at Banff and Lake Louise, the golf course, the three ski hills, the 200 miles (320 kilometers) of roads, 1,000 miles (1,600 kilometers) of foot trails, and all the outlying commercial establishments and campgrounds have fragmented the wildlife habitat, threatened genetic dispersal, and increased the conflict between wildlife and humans. Elk have moved into the town to escape from cougars and wolves; people who approach them too closely for snapshots have been injured. Elk, largest of the deer family after the moose, can cut a person wide open with their split hooves. The warden service has been trapping and relocating elk to reduce their numbers. Recently, hungry cougars and wolves have begun moving into town looking for urban elk meat. Eight cougars and eighteen wolves killed about a hundred elk in 2000, taking down some animals on the fairways of the Banff Springs golf course. Now that they are getting lean and hungry, wolves are stealing elk kills from cougars and the big cats are getting desperate. A local woman, Frances Frost, was killed by a cougar in 2001 while cross-country skiing near the town, and the residents now fear for the safety of their children.

Experts believe the damage could spread to the entire park system. The 1996 Bow Valley Study asserted: "Most parks in southern Canada are losing ecological integrity and will require increasing levels of active management."

The wonder is not that sublime landscapes are threatened; the wonder is that Parks Canada, with all the handicaps it has had to carry, has done such a good job protecting park lands and acquiring new ones in recent years. This is a tribute to the principled, dedicated people spread throughout the organization. Parks Canada has been kicked around like a soccer ball in the past two decades. It was moved from the Department of Indian Affairs and Northern Development—always an odd fit—into the Department of the Environment, then into the Department of Canadian Heritage, where it finally morphed (in 1998) into the Parks Canada Agency, a crown corporation run by a CEO, Tom Lee, formerly assistant deputy minister of Parks Canada.

In the 1980s, a Liberal minister, the Honourable Suzanne Blais-Grenier, talked openly about allowing mining and logging in the national parks, causing a national uproar. The Honourable Tom McMillan, bolstered by environmentalists, finally took a stand and introduced a key amendment into the National Parks Act in 1988. "Maintenance of Ecological Integrity through the protection of natural resources shall be the first priority when considering park zoning and visitor use in a management plant." Conservationists had been waiting years to hear those words.

The ministry changed hands in 1993. Parks Canada suffered budget cuts in the 1980s and an additional 24 percent cut in 1995 that has yet to be restored. Under the burden of national debt, the language of business crept in to everyday thinking. The park interpretive service, which was set up to educate the "clients" on conservation values, was gutted and basically silenced. Through-out the system, support services were cut. The science program, vital for advancing ecological integrity, went begging for funds. Senior wardens and park interpreters were offered buyout pack-ages; they took with them decades of experience, knowledge, and hard-to-learn skills.

The wonderful system of 39 national parks preserves sub-lime landscapes and fascinating wildlife, but they are no longer a priceless, public trust. They are becoming a business with a mar-keting arm focused on wealthy "clients." They are becoming the paradise of the middle class. In this era of the $70 (Canadian) entry permit, parks must "recoup the treasury." And now, more than ever, the "doubtful class" of poorer Canadians can't afford the price of admission.

The Parks Canada hierarchy that Minister Sheila Copps inherited in 1995 was a wounded beast. Minister Copps promised to curb the commercialization of Banff, of capping its retail space and its population. She was going to shut down the park airport, which was disrupting the movements of wildlife down the Cascade River Valley. Wildlife underpasses in the twinned highway, fenced off in 1979 to reduce roadkills, were supposed to let the animals move freely through their range, but female grizzlies would have no part of them. The minister decided to approve, at a cost of four million dollars (Canadian), two grizzly bear overpasses. Development would be capped on all three ski resorts in Banff.

In 1997, the minister imposed a one-year moratorium on development in the park. But in 1998, Minister Copps approved a seven-story, 156,000-square-foot meeting facility at Lake Louise. The minister's decision to approve a convention center on the shores of a world heritage site is a throwback to the old business as usual era of Banff Park. Environmentalists fear even more people will flood into the already crowded landscape, forcing the wildlife out altogether.

The EI panel of experts commissioned by Parks Canada reported its findings in the year 2000. The panel found that the ecological integrity of all 39 national parks was under threat from both external and internal sources. The panel studied shortcomings and offered a comprehensive blueprint for managing, planning, protection, and interpretation. The panel urged the agency to undo the damage of the past two decades; to phase out inappropriate uses and facilities; to make ecological integrity the core concept of all planning; and to rebuild the scientific and park interpretive functions to research the needs and communicate the values of ecological integrity. It challenged the agency to reach out beyond its borders to garner support from provincial agencies in protecting common interests. And most important, it told the agency that Parks Canada never had a dual mandate to begin with. "Parks staff must receive a clear signal and acknowledge that there is no dual mandate but rather one single mandate. Parks are places for the protection of ecological integrity and for visitors to experience and enjoy in a manner that leaves ecological integrity unimpaired."

From our human perspective, perhaps the most valuable quality of sublime landscapes is solitude, a quality in decreasing supply throughout the urbanized world today. The absence of distraction engendered by solitude encourages contemplation of the beautiful or awe-inspiring, and that act of contemplation slows down time itself, as if a great wheel, somewhere in the firmament, had shifted into low gear. In a time of change for the sake of change, the ability to slow down and savor our lives is a great gift. Naturalists have known this since the time of Thoreau and Muir. It was eloquently expressed decades ago by J.B. Harkin. "People sometimes accuse me of being a mystic about the influences of the mountains," he said. "Perhaps I am. I devoutly believe that there are emanations from them, intangible but very real, which elevate the mind and purify the spirit."

But this solitude is easily compromised. Is a mountain a sublime or extreme landscape if it exists in entirety, with its ecosystems intact; or is it wild, and therefore sublime, only above the zone of human development? Is the European model of extreme landscapes suitable for North America? Which of these two definitions does the public find more desirable—the solitary mountain as its own entity or the human-engineered mountain?

Many years ago, J. B. Harkin looked into the future and wrote these words: "The day will come, when the population of Canada will be ten times as great as it is now, but the National Parks ensure that every Canadian, by right of citizenship, will still have free access to vast areas in which the beauty of the landscape is protected from profanation, the natural wild animals, plants and forests preserved, and the peace and solitude of primeval nature retained."

That right is threatened. The future of the sublime landscape lies first and foremost in our aspirations for it. Step forward from the solitudes, you that love the sublime, and if only for a moment, let a great voice that cannot speak for itself infuse you and become your voice.

Let it be heard.

Galway Bay, Ireland SAM ABELL

dumbstruck ✳ DERMOT SOMERS

AN OLD MAN WAS KILLED at a bend on the coast road three miles out of Ballyvaughan in County Clare, in the west of Ireland—not the only bend on this winding Atlantic road that hugs the shore of Galway Bay and then swings sharply south through Fanore, past the hidden crag at Ailladie, to Lisdoonvarna, Doolin, and the Cliffs of Moher.

The twisted road, looking west over the ocean to the Aran Islands, outlines one of the most intensely cultured limestone areas in the world—the Burren, in County Clare. *Boireann* in Irish is an old and resonant term, a rocky place.

At daybreak, a dark sky behind it to the north, the limestone gleams with a silvery sheen: tides of geology frozen in layers above the swelling and falling sea. At a distance the plateau is a bare canvas, apart from hazel scrub, thickets of sloe, briars, ivy pencil-shading the contours. Close up, the Burren flora is dazzlingly diverse—mountain avens, maidenhair fern, helleborines, gentians, orchids—arctic-alpine to Mediterranean. The unique mélange might be a symbol of the different races that seeded this landscape with their presence over 6,000 or 7,000 years.

The first few millennia are mute, the soundtrack lost. We don't know who they were, or what they spoke, or how they named the landscape. The wind, sighing among stones, remembers nothing. They left their ciphers on the rock, their tombs across the plateau. But they do not speak to us.

Three thousand years ago, or thereabouts, the people loosely known as Celts emerged in Ireland, and from that vague point on we hear a whisper rising from the past, and then the mumble of myth, murmur of poem, drone of law-text, prayer.

We hack back and forward through thickets of words. We send out signals; bounce echoes off the evidence. We recognize key words in the oldest texts. So, the Irish we speak is still in some sense theirs. That much at least. It hangs on against crushing, modern odds, refusing to die in spite of centuries of colonization, poverty, emigration. Some say it's already dead: just won't shut up.

To reach back through language, looking for our origins, is to cup the hands in a funnel and shout, and when the shout returns, distorted, a conversation with our earlier selves goes on. Theirs was an Indo-European language, which we can discern: Our speech derives from it. It's in the landscape and the weather, the crops and animals they raised. Their elemental words are seeded throughout the ancient tongues of Europe and further back, to Sanskrit. They occur in our earliest documents, from the fifth century A.D. The words are still there in the modern Irish tongue—*marcach*, *ag marcaíocht*, from *marc*, an Indo-European horse.

Speech adapted to the contours of the landscape, conditions of the habitat, the nature of the work. So, our language is a verbal map of our present place, how we arrived, and where we were along the way. Without it, we would be in a real sense alien, adrift.

At the bend that I've already mentioned on the Ballyvaughan road, an old man, walking, was knocked down by a car some years ago and killed. He was the last native speaker of West Clare Gaelic, born into an unbroken web of language and local landscape. A different kind of voice, an older one, has quietly gone out. The collision was only cruel emphasis. Had he died in bed, he was still the last one of his kind.

Today that coast is a tourist belt and everyone there speaks English. They live in a mesh of place-names, a web of references, cultural coordinates, anglicized, unintelligible. Houses and villages are lit at night for security, and TVs rattle with a mid-Atlantic babble, glowing with the phosphorescence of a mysterious decay. Irish is taught in schools, broadcast on TV, spoken by some individuals, but it is not the language that grew into that landscape long ago. It is a graft, a second skin.

All over the world these voices are dying; memories, identities, are fading unnoticed, leaving shadows, blankness, patches of silence behind. The consequence is loss—of knowledge, wisdom, identity. But in a broader sense, broader than language, the greatest loss is the simple fact that ancestral voices are being stilled.

There are different kinds of death. The worst, the most complete, ends in deadly silence in some high place where people struggled to survive enormous odds and no trace of their lives remains, no echo of their voices, songs, meanings, their naming of hard-won place and pasture. Language in the broadest sense is a gift to the future, a memorial to the past.

Aside from religion, this promise is our defense against death. The silence in that lost place is more than death: It is extinction.

According to the ethnologue of SIL (the Summer Institute of Linguistics), there are 6,800 languages in the world today. Within the lifespan of a single generation half of these languages will decline beyond recovery. Thus, in this decade, in the golden age of communication, half of the languages in the world have entered the shadow of extinction. These languages will soon have no young native speakers at all. They will then be moribund, spoken only by elder speakers whose demise will mean extinction. Each one reaches its bend in the road, around which lies oblivion. These are not merely regional dialects with an accent and a local flavor as West Clare Gaelic was; these are complete languages, separate, distinguishable.

Going further, linguists have posed basic standards—numbers of speakers, official support—that might assure the survival of a language for a while. Applying these practical standards, it appears that of the 6,800 languages still alive, over 90 percent will not survive this century.

If this degree of attrition occurred at an environmental level, it would be seen as a global emergency. There are practical policies for intervention afoot, languages chosen for UN support, but there is no real sense of crisis. In the case of a dying language it is usually too late for intensive care, mouth-to-mouth resuscitation.

The first thing to offer is respect. Languages are not dying because they are worthless—they die because they are delicate and in difficult circumstances. Many people regard such a rate of extinction as a sign of progress, a rationalization, lopping off dead wood to encourage central stems. But it doesn't work like that. Language is a root, not a branch.

There is a unique situation in Ireland, where the older language, Gaelic/Irish, is the official first language, state-supported. It endures constant hostility from monoglot Anglophiles for its brazen refusal to die. English is almost universally spoken and is the language of commerce and communication, while Irish maintains a persistent low-key strength, an aspirational presence, in the hearts if not in the mouths of the public.

Critics may hector a language, shout it down, bully it into a stammer, but a much more effective veto is exercised by children. In a culture divided or confused over speech, children can and do make the final choice to reject one tongue wholly and adopt another, while the elders stand by, struck dumb.

Children have this extraordinary power, since they do not merely receive language: They re-create it in a process that is still poorly understood. They are exercising their veto today in languages such as the Yupik tongue in certain areas of Alaska; in Khaling Rai in eastern Nepal; in Gaelic on the Aran Islands; Nenets, in Arctic Siberia. But it is not a deliberate choice: They do not control the initial judgment. Their decisions are formed by external forces, cultural and economic.

In disadvantaged areas these values are often formed by parents who see their own language and identity as a barrier to progress and turn their children away from it toward the language of economic power. As with any form of betrayal forced upon decent people, this process requires that they stigmatize something in order to absolve themselves of shame. The native language bears the brunt, becoming a sign of ignorance, a perceived impediment to progress.

In many cases they have a point. The language of a culture in social and economic decline becomes a feature of that decline, locking its speakers into a descending spiral of exclusion. The language itself begins to atrophy as the imaginative dynamic falters. It comes to represent backward values, lacking the vocabulary to deal with a more technical world. I'm occasionally asked: What's the point of Irish—apart from counting our cows? Although the elite in a multilingual culture will usually despise the weakest tongue, no one despises it as much as the native speaker eager to scrape it off his shoes and join the elite.

A major culprit in the extinction of language is the kind of national politics that sees unity in terms of a national language, a single identity, a uniform culture. In order to have access to power, you must speak the language of power. The more exclusively you speak it, the more clearly you will be heard.

The European Union has attempted to avoid such stereotyping with initial attempts at parity of language. This may well be an unspoken reason why Britain is such a reluctant participant. A democracy of tongues was intolerable during the spread of English as an imperial language, and parity is also anathema to the further spread of Anglo-American as the vehicle of global culture.

But the main culprit in the death of language is the economic force with a style and a product to sell and a seductive language in which to sell it. The most remote cultures of the Earth, those of the great mountain ranges, have been penetrated, riddled even, by Anglo-American language and culture, products and values. All the villages of the world have become a single market for sugary drinks and snacks. Not only do the teeth rot, so does the tongue.

Tragic for the victims; sad in an utterly different sense for people like myself. English is the language I speak, read, and write primarily, a language I admire for its richness and flexibility, and simultaneously fear for its omnivorous destructiveness, its innate hostility to any language other than itself. A force unleashed by empire as part of its arsenal, it has gone on to assert its own far greater imperial reach as the language of expansion and consumption.

English itself, mainstream Anglo-American, has grown baggy and loose in recent decades with the explosion of internal sub-languages—technical-write, economic jargon, tabloidism, sport-speak, etc.—drawing energy from the core language and returning it, dissipated. However, this degeneracy is more than counteracted by the flow of powerful energies, narrative, poetical, rhetorical, from the margins—Ireland, India, Africa, the Caribbean—former colonies, revitalizing the language while, incidentally, extending the range of its destruction.

✳

I HAVE WALKED MANY TIMES through Solu-Khumbu with my friend Dhan Bahadur Rai, who comes from the village of Phuleli, high on the upper slopes of the Dudh Khosi River in eastern Nepal. Khaling is his language and culture. Mountains are a commonplace seen from his home. Numbur is the local peak; the school playground of beaten, red earth (girls playing volleyball in the yard) frames an entire face of Kusum Kanguru in the distance; Kangtega is in the view from Phuleli; the eye can't avoid Tamserku's icy wedge...

We've been up and down the trails together. We babble away, going back over words and sentences like missed views, reconstructing them, telling stories, explaining similarities, differences, discussing ideas. Half my age, he asks questions with too much respect. My voice grows irritable, protesting equality.

When I'm not here to see the changing landscape, he keeps me posted. "The summer has dressed the hills and terraces of farm fields with its colorful greeneries. The younghood of summer can be seen with the movement of rivers and streams flowing in their own motion and speed freedomly in accordance with the form of surfaces."

I used to wonder if there was a danger that he'd pick up our rose-tinted, pearl-hued Western perspective and reflect it back, or if this formal sense of the Earth and its weather is actually embodied in the English language as gleaned from schoolbooks and recommended poetry.

But it's the enthusiasm of rediscovery that's being expressed. Dhana and his generation had gone in high excitement to the big city, to Kathmandu, not as laborers but as students, and had been swallowed up. When they escaped the polluted valley to go home, they saw the highlands with newly opened eyes. Mountain languages, while minutely descriptive of the home landscape in its every detail, do not lend themselves to that modern sense of loss and rediscovery, of alienation and reintegration, the expression of the rural/urban divide, in the way that modern literary languages do—languages that have grappled with the breakdown of identity over a couple of centuries and have crystallized the fragments into ready sentiment.

Quite apart from economic attraction, the imagination is drawn toward languages that recognize individual rather than tribal thinking. This should be a healthy process. The crucial point is not to reject the native language (Khaling, Sherpa, Tamang, Newari, Thakali) in this shift, but to retain it as a foundation and a strength, a local voice that may at different times be an echo, in harmony, an argument, a shout, a punch line, a welcome home.

Mountains are a repository of language and vocabulary, practical and expressive, not only in place names but in the functions of the land itself—in the expression of an authentic way of life. Such functions have seasonal rhythms and geographical fixity, and they root the identity in the working reality of the landscape, while at the same time reflecting that landscape in the imagination. Out of this interplay comes richness of thought and word. Such vocabulary, such language, is fundamental to the sense of place and of identity that acts like a gyroscope to keep a people balanced. A culture no longer pegged in place by such reference points is a slack tent in a storm.

Dhana is a community-man, an idealist who believes in language, education, culture, and environment with an innocence I never had—or lost so long ago that I don't remember it. Small and energetic, with considerable strength, he has a history of personal effort against the odds. Life has not hardened his personality; it has sensitized him, made him humorous, versatile. He has been a cultural guide in a land of tribes and tongues.

There are 120 languages in Nepal. Nepali itself is the first language of ten million speakers, about half the population. It is one of the Indo-Aryan tongues that entered more or less from the south and are usually associated with Hinduism. A group of Tibeto-Burman languages spread roughly from the opposite direction, bringing with them Buddhism and various tribal religions.

In the wider world, the best known of the Tibeto-Burman languages is Sherpa, which surprisingly, despite its profile, has no more than 50,000 speakers. In eastern Nepal, most of the Tibeto-Burman languages are loosely grouped as Rai. Numbers vary, but when all the languages of the Rai group are added together, the total is approximately 400,000 speakers. These languages are largely independent and are, generally speaking, not mutually intelligible. Dhana's language, Khaling Rai, has 12,000 speakers, a dangerously low total. Khulung and Thulung are in a similar position, and Vayu is now extinct.

To many Nepalese, the landscape is a matter of fact, just as the Connemara mountains are a matter of fact to an Irish sheep farmer. From the very beginning, Dhana displayed a response to language, music, and landscape that was genuinely refreshing. With him, you felt he was as deeply moved by his own country as you were. He had a headful of English words and grammar that he put together slowly, carefully; a concern for syntax that worried you listening, in case it might hinder his ability to communicate to his own advantage with that happy-go-lucky inventiveness of Nepali staff. Far less thoughtful speakers will rattle off shallow explanations to please tourists in the demotic English that comes so easily to versatile Nepalis accustomed to multilingualism.

He would stand at the end of the dinner table in the mess tent, when I bullied him to speak, looking at once adult and childlike, after the *chai* and biscuits were served and the cards shuffled for stud poker, and deliver a careful speech about local culture, which, if it was naive, was distinguished by the shy pride and the lyrical locutions that accompanied it. He sang too (although he insisted that he didn't, that it wasn't singing) and played the flute, taking my pennywhistle and squeezing bendy Himalayan melody out of it that I never knew it contained. We rehearsed each other's songs and sang them together year after year. My pronunciation was poor and there was entertainment to be had from accidental meanings. On the other hand, he understood the Irish song "Will ye go, Lassie, go?" as an invitation to share a milkshake, a banana *lassi.*

With other Nepalese, indeed any nationality, there is a warmth and affability, but it has its limits. They will turn to each other to laugh and talk and you've lost them: they've gone home without you. With Dhana it was never like that. We were part of the same community, like-minded, linked by an emotional sense of culture and landscape that set us apart from our friends, a sense that we had something important to learn from each other and to teach. Except that it would not be teaching—it would be communication.

We walked together a part of every day through the foothills of Solu. On Trakshindo Pass we picked our way over the watershed, past a weathered stupa, prayer flags streaming under high cirrus, torn veils of the highland sky, through swarms of flowers, velvet funnels full of a blue so blue it went past color into content. "Trumpet-gentian" became a code for exactitude of naming, cropping up again and again in unexpected ground for a decade; as did "dereliction" in a different context when we stood among the broken huts of an abandoned village where water had ceased to flow. I entered a tumbledown house and thought, *riclín tí,* in an island language full of broken walls and roofs by the western ocean. Dhana had words for the dereliction in at least two languages besides English—to which he carefully added "dilapidation," practicing it throughout the afternoon for the enjoyment of the syllabic rattle.

As we walked and talked our way toward Khumbu that first time, along the gorge of the Dudh Khosi, watching mountains of ice form like premonitions above the terraced foothills, I picked up threads of his earliest journey along the route. At the age of ten or so, Dhana had traveled with his father and other farmers on a trading trip to the Sherpa market in Namcha Bazar, several days away and many thousands of feet above their own hills. They had been barefoot, of course, carrying precious 60-pound loads of maize, barley, and millet slung on their backs. These were long journeys making very little profit, as if trade were its own dynamic. They would return with a handful of rupees, with cloth, paraffin, necessities.

To a small boy from far away, Namcha Bazar, the Sherpa capital, was a babble of raucous languages, frightening, fascinating, a press of bodies in fibrous clothes, a crush of highland beasts, stew of savors and stenches, paved alleys and crowded spaces where Tibetan traders in rawhide coats with long, black, oily hair sold anything from Buddhist treasures to salt-butter. Sherpas roistered on *rakshi* in their own hometown like Kerry farmers at Puck Fair. Tired stubbled men, Rai farmers, who had traveled far with precious little and might go home with less, had a worn look in their red-rimmed eyes and a stumble in their gait. If they knocked back rakshi to harden themselves, they took on the rawness of dispossession.

When I was a boy, we sold a few cattle from time to time at a street fair in Roscommon town, a place so low in the landscape it may be below sea level. I helped herd them along the country roads in the middle of the night, chasing them out of bog and commonage to arrive on the streets at dawn and take up a position at the curb in front of some boarded-up huckster's shop, or a pub with sawdust on the floor and the bitter smell of porter, sour as nettle juice. Dealers came by, cold-eyed, red-faced, in peaked caps and heavy coats with blackthorn sticks, boots covered in cow shit, bullying, haggling. Once, a bullock shouldered its way into the hall past a woman who opened her front door onto the street. The unfortunate beast was beaten back out with a sweeping brush, and I pretended he wasn't in my care.

Everyone spoke English: colorful, uncouth variations full of the sly immediacy of trade, accents that bore the shape of the Gaelic that had been spat aside a century before. And yet the tribes of us were still clearly distinguishable, audible, if one had the ear—the bogmen, the canny dealers, strong farmers, townsmen, tinkers. By now, the distinctions are blurred. We've merged into the anonymity of international trade, boom and recession, and the flight from the land and language. No one would want to have retained the squalor and hardship, however colorful. But who would choose to arrive where we are at present, a bubble of technology dependent on world trade in computers and mobile phones?

Dhana grew serious, not angry but exercised, when he talked of social justice. I sensed how the structures of power might shut the people out, the knuckles of the mountains clenched into a fist against them. He was painfully aware of inequality, whether in land rights, in education and employment, in gender issues, in the starvation wages of laborers and porters, or the pittance paid to teachers working in hovels.

Testing his ideas on me, he was finding a common language for them, and I affirmed his beliefs from my own experience. If they were naive I didn't say so. He had a policy, an approach, a personal commitment to improve things for his community. Later, we prompted Irish funding that sent him to college in Kathmandu, where he trained as a teacher while continuing to work in trekking. That was where an unequal society showed itself most sharply. Despite his commitment to return to the highlands, to improve things through education, he couldn't afford to do so, given the dependence of an extended family and the low wages of a rural teacher.

And so he expressed his commitment through volunteer work on educational and cultural issues. He played a fundamental role over several demanding years in establishing a new local school and children's playground in land-hungry Phuleli, donating family property as a site. That campaign in itself generated a new cultural dynamic in the community, which is being harnessed for further projects.

I suppose I taught him a measure of English over a decade or so, a few weeks at a time. He already had a second language, Nepali, which in its own way as the language of the Brahmin-Chhetri, the Hindu cultural and political elite, is pushing minority languages to the wall. He was in no doubt that he needed English in order to extend himself, just as he needed IT skills and acquired them too.

I was keen to understand how he felt about his native tongue, Khaling, surrounded by economically stronger languages— Sherpa, Nepali, English. Was it a cul-de-sac, a drawback, a hindrance, a sign of backwardness or ignorance?

Far from it. Khaling Rai is his identity: It tells him what and who he is. It identifies his community, their traditions, their resources, and their needs. As a cultured community it is their most valued possession; without it they lose their individuality, their stories and songs, their traditions, their racial memory. Without it, he says, he cannot honor his ancestors.

Through the experience of the Irish language, I thought I understood the nature of this belonging, the peculiar succor-and-pull of a root system overgrown and tangled but still feeding that older tree in the forest, which every now and then catches the weather in a way that shows its native strength, its shelter, its consonance with the landscape.

But it's secondhand in my case. I learned my native language in school. It had died out in my area a hundred years before I was born. Colonization wore it down, the Famine stuffed its mouth with grass and clay. It is back now, a ghost of itself, thinly, painfully restored, transparent, dilute, but still preciously rooted. And it has grafted onto modern life: literature, television.

Still, today I'm a detached citizen of a postmodern world, peripatetic, transcultural, attached to an idea of language rather than a reality. Anglo-American charges my daily imagination; Irish is a reacquisition, at once a cultural construct and an atrophied memory. There was a period of dispossession, enforced amnesia.

We've lost our indigenous forests too: The oak and the elm are gone. It occurs to me as a secondhand Gaelic speaker that I'm more like a telegraph pole planted in woodland than a native tree. I recognize the kinship of timber, sense it in the ground, but I'm not rooted that way. I'm upside down, rooted in the air, part of the new order, wired to the world for sound.

It's not like that yet for hill people in Asia, Africa, South America. Their heads may be in the clouds from our perspective, but they are still grounded in their earth by language and tradition.

To Dhana, Khaling Rai is still a daily reality, the language of home, of aged parents, neighbors; Khaling is the medium that fits the animals to the fields, the millet, barley, and maize to the ground, the snow to the mountains, the songs to their melodies.

He does not think it will survive his generation.

Mt. Sinai summit EDWIN BERNBAUM

mountains of inspiration ✳ EDWIN BERNBAUM

MOUNTAINS HAVE THE POWER to move us in a multitude of mysterious ways. A glimpse of pale blue ranges on the far horizon can revive longings for dimly remembered places of childhood fantasy. A gleam of gold on a distant peak can evoke visions of divine beauty and splendor. The lift of a ridge against a bright sky can send our spirits soaring toward luminous heights. The rough touch of cold rock can elicit a sense of direct contact with the concrete reality of a cliff or mountain looming over us. The crunch of snow beneath our boots can awaken us to the sharp freshness of a new day. The infinite circle of a summit view can open us to a vaster universe encompassing the limited world of our ordinary lives.

Because of their evocative nature, mountains have come to reflect some of the deepest values and highest aspirations of cultures throughout the world. The Bible singles out Mount Sinai as the awe-inspiring place where Moses received the Ten Commandments. Looming over the plateau of western Tibet, the remote peak of Mount Kailas inspires millions of Hindus and Buddhists with the aspiration to attain the heights of spiritual liberation. The perfect cone of Mount Fuji embodies the quest for beauty and simplicity that lies at the heart of Japanese culture. For many in modern society, nonclimbers as well as climbers, the summit of Everest symbolizes their highest goals and the dedication needed to achieve them.

From the Rockies to the Himalaya, people around the world look to mountains as sources of meaning, renewal, wisdom, creativity, and vision. Well-known sages, poets, writers, artists, and climbers have all drawn inspiration from the heights. An exploration of how some of the most beautiful and uplifting places on Earth have inspired these figures can help to tap similar sources of inspiration in our own lives—places of inner experience that have the power to transform our views of ourselves and the world around us. This kind of inspiration can be the personal, spiritual meaning of mountains, as exemplified in the images and words of the photographer Ansel Adams, who wrote in his autobiography:

> *No matter how sophisticated you may be, a large granite mountain cannot be denied—it speaks in silence to the very core of your being. There are some that care not to listen but the disciples are drawn to the high altar with magnetic certainty, knowing that a great Presence hovers over the ranges.*

Or this exploration may have a value for society as a whole; William O. Douglas, justice of the U.S. Supreme Court, stated:

> *A people who climb the ridges and sleep under the stars in high mountain meadows, who enter the forest and scale peaks, who explore glaciers and walk ridges buried deep in snow—these people will give their country some of the indomitable spirit of the mountains.*

※

THROUGHOUT HISTORY, in many parts of the world, sages have sought out mountains as sources of wisdom and transformation. The ancient Chinese regarded misty peaks as such ideal places for pursuing spiritual practices leading to immortality and enlightenment that the expression for embarking on a religious path means literally "to enter the mountains." This idea was so deeply ingrained that the word for "sage" is composed of two characters that stand for "man" and "mountain," so that a sage is literally a "mountain man." Many Indian nations in North America, particularly those living in the Plains and Rocky Mountains, regard mountains as sites of particular power for engaging in vision quests. On the open summit of a hill or mountain, a young person will cry for a vision that will reveal his guiding spirit and show him the course of his life. Orthodox Christian monks and hermits seek to become one with the uncreated light of God on the lonely heights of mountains such as Mount Athos in Greece.

No mountain in Japan is more closely linked with the life of one person than is Mount Koya with Kobo Daishi, also known as Kukai, the founder of Shingon or Esoteric Japanese Buddhism.

Kobo Daishi was a gifted philosopher, artist, poet, engineer, and writer, as well as a great religious leader. Born into a noble family in A.D. 773, he left his aristocratic life to become a wandering monk.

Kobo Daishi regarded mountains as the ideal places to find freedom of spirit, as his description of himself attests: "The blue sky was the ceiling of his hut and the clouds hanging over the mountains were his curtains; he did not need to worry about where he lived or where he slept. In summer he opened his neck band in a relaxed mood and delighted in the gentle breezes as though he were a great king ... he wandered throughout the country like duckweed floating on water or dry grass blown by the wind."

Kobo Daishi's wanderings took him to China in search of Buddhist teachings. According to legend, at the end of his stay there, he hurled a three-pronged *vajra* or diamond thunderbolt toward Japan with the prayer that it would show him a place to establish a center of spiritual practice. When he went to look for it on his return, he met a hunter with two dogs, who revealed himself as a hunting god and offered to guide him to the spot. His dogs led Kobo Daishi to the vajra hidden on a forested plateau on top of Mount Koya. The goddess of the mountain, who was also the mother of the hunting god, gave him permission to construct a monastery there.

At the time Koya was a mountain wilderness where Kobo Daishi had meditated as a youth. He wrote a letter to the emperor of Japan asking to build a monastery on the mountain, not only for religion but also for the sake of the nation as well. Granted permission, Kobo Daishi sent disciples ahead and came to the sacred mountain two years later. The beautiful poetry he composed there reflects his deep feelings for nature and the renewal that he experienced in his mountain retreat:

Spring flowers and autumn chrysanthemums smile upon me;
The moon at dawn and the breezes at morn cleanse my heart.

Kobo Daishi passed away on his beloved mountain and his body was buried in a beautiful forest of cedars. A tradition arose that he had not actually died, but had instead gone into a state of suspended animation, awaiting the coming of the next Buddha. A vast cemetery, the largest in Japan, grew up around the site so that people could have their remains interred in the presence of Kobo Daishi, where his spirit could continue to guide them, even in death.

Tibet's most famous yogi, Milarepa, lived in the 11th and 12th centuries and spent much of his life meditating high in the Himalaya, wearing only a cotton shirt and practicing a yoga that kept him warm by generating body heat. He was drawn, in particular, to Mount Kailas, an isolated peak in western Tibet revered as the most sacred mountain in the world by Tibetan Buddhists, Hindus, and followers of the indigenous Tibetan tradition of Bon. When Milarepa arrived at the foot of Kailas, the local Bon priest, Naro Bhun Chon, insisted he would have to convert to Bon if he wished to meditate there. Milarepa refused and Naro challenged him to a series of miracle contests to determine whose religion would prevail in the region. The final contest was a race to the top of Kailas.

Early before dawn on the appointed day, Naro flew off on his shaman's drum toward the summit. Milarepa, who had overslept, made a gesture of power, and the Bon priest found himself circling around the peak, unable to go higher. Then, with a snap of a finger, Milarepa went straight to the summit of Kailas in one of the most elegant ascents in mountaineering history. Astonished to see his rival perched on the summit above him, Naro fell off his drum; it tumbled down the south face of Kailas, leaving a central couloir with a series of indentations that Hindus view as a stairway leading to heaven.

One of Milarepa's many songs of spiritual accomplishment expresses some of the ways in which the mountain inspired his efforts to attain the ultimate Buddhist goal of enlightenment:

> *The prophecy of Buddha says most truly,*
> *That this snow mountain is the center of the world,*
> *A place where the snow leopards dance.*
> *...*
>
> *This is the great place of accomplished yogis;*
> *Here one attains transcendent accomplishments.*
> *There is no place more wonderful than this,*
> *There is no place more marvelous than here.*

Mountains have played—and continue to play—important roles in the visions and vision quests of American Plains Indians, as evidenced in the life of Black Elk, a Lakota medicine man. At the age of nine, he had a vision in which he was taken up to the sky to meet the six Grandfathers in a teepee made of rainbows roofed with clouds. These powers of the six directions, who represented Wakan Tanka or the Great Spirit, gave him the power to heal and lead his people through the terrible times ahead. At the end of the vision, the cloud teepee changed:

I heard a voice saying: "Look back and behold it." I looked back and the cloud house was gone. There was nothing but a big mountain with a gap in it.

That mountain, according to Black Elk, was Pikes Peak in the Colorado Rockies. Seen in the distance from the Great Plains where the Lakota roamed, it looks like a great cloud of snow and hazy rock.

Earlier in the vision, his spirit guides took him to another mountain and said, "Behold the center of the Earth for we are taking you there." Black Elk describes what he saw from there: "As I looked I could see great mountains with rocks and forests on them. I could see all colors of light flashing out of the mountains toward the four quarters. Then they took me on top of a high mountain where I could see all over the earth." From this high point he looked down on the world of suffering and joy. The peak to which Black Elk went in his vision he later identified as Harney Peak, the highest summit of the Black Hills, an isolated range of mountains sacred to the Sioux. In his old age, having witnessed the destruction of his people and culture, Black Elk returned to the mountain of his childhood vision. Standing on the summit of Harney Peak, convinced that he had failed, he extended his arms and cried out: "In sorrow I am sending a voice, O six powers of the earth, hear me in sorrow. With tears I am sending a voice. May you behold me and hear me that my people may live again."

Perhaps the most famous ascent of a mountain is Moses' climb of Mount Sinai to receive the first five books of the Bible and the Ten Commandments. The Book of Exodus describes it in this way:

> *Now Mount Sinai was altogether on a smoke,*
> *because the Lord descended upon it in fire; and the*
> *smoke thereof ascended as the smoke of a furnace,*
> *and the whole mount quaked greatly. And when the*
> *voice of the horn waxed louder and louder, Moses*
> *spoke, and God answered him by a voice. And the*
> *Lord came down upon Mount Sinai, to the top of*
> *the Mount: and the Lord called Moses to the top of*
> *the mount; and Moses went up.*

Whether or not it actually happened, the dramatic story of Moses' ascent has had an enormous historical impact. The Ten Commandments that he was said to have brought down from the mountain form the basis for much of law and ethics in Western civilization. The revelation and covenant at Mount Sinai are considered the single most important event in traditional Jewish history.

We often think of the Western approach to climbing as conquering a mountain, but here, in an account that informs much of Western thought, there is no idea of conquest: Moses climbs Mount Sinai in response to a call in order to receive something of benefit for others. The summit of the mountain is the meeting place of the human and the divine. Indeed, Moses is regarded in Jewish tradition as the greatest of all the prophets because he alone comes face to face with God—on the heights of Mount Sinai—and comes down transfigured, his face shining with light.

The passage focuses not on the mountain, which it hardly describes, but on its transformation: the fire and smoke that envelop the peak to reveal the awesome presence of God. Moses first experiences this kind of transformation in the episode of the burning bush at the foot of Mount Sinai. Like the mountain, the bush burns with a miraculous fire that reveals the presence of God. In both cases a feature of the natural landscape becomes a conduit of supernatural power and glory, a means by which man becomes aware of the divine. Many of us experience something similar, on a lesser scale, when we turn on a trail and a shaft of sunlight strikes a peak or tree and it seems to come alive with a beauty and meaning that pierce the heart.

*

LIKE SAGES, poets and writers have long been drawn to the heights. Beginning around the fourth century, Chinese literati sought relief from the stultifying confines of the imperial court, going up into mountains for renewal and composing poetry based on their experiences there. In fact, mountain climbing as a form of recreation began in China more than a thousand years before the birth of Alpinism in Europe. Only with the advent of the Enlightenment and romanticism in the 18th and early 19th centuries did Europeans turn to mountains for sport and literary inspiration. Since then, numerous poets and novelists such as William Wordsworth and Thomas Mann have composed works based on the power of mountains to move the human spirit and evoke a sense of the sublime.

The Chinese poet Li Po, who lived in the eighth century, loved to wander among mountains, seeking out the company of hermits. One of his poems reads:

> *Up high all the birds have flown away,*
> *A single cloud drifts off across the sky.*
> *We settle down together, never tiring of each other,*
> *Only the two of us, the mountain and I.*

The poem expresses a sense of quiet communion between peak and poet. Through this communion with the mountain, he becomes one with the Tao, the spiritual essence of reality that one can experience in nature.

Like Li Po, the Japanese master of haiku, Basho, loved to roam mountains, where he also meditated with hermits. One of his most famous works, *The Narrow Road to the North*, describes a journey he took in 1689 through the northern part of Honshu, the main island of Japan. Along the way he visited shrines at many sacred mountains. This is how he describes his ascent of one of these peaks, Gas-san, or Moon Mountain:

I walked through mists and clouds, breathing the thin air of high altitudes and stepping on slippery ice and snow, till at last through a gateway of clouds, as it seemed, to the very paths of the sun and moon, I reached the summit, completely out of breath and nearly frozen to death.

The passage blends the physical experience of mountain climbing with a vision of transcendence, of paths that continue beyond the top of the peak, up to the divine realm of the sun and moon.

Basho opens *The Records of a Weather-Exposed Skeleton*, an account of another walking trip, with a haiku that singles out Mount Fuji's elusiveness as one of its main attractions:

Delightful, in a way,
to miss seeing Mount Fuji
In the misty rain.

For Basho and many others, mountains like Fuji embody a presence that can be felt even when the peak itself is hidden from view.

During the 18th century, the writings of the French-Swiss philosopher and novelist Jean-Jacques Rousseau played a major role in transforming European attitudes toward mountains. His novel *La Nouvelle Héloïse* probably did more than any other single work of literature to awaken enthusiasm for the Alps. One particularly influential passage describes the beneficial effects of climbing a mountain:

It was there that I visibly discerned…the true cause of the change in my mood, and the return of the inner peace that I had lost for so long.… on high mountains, where the air is pure and subtle, one feels greater ease in breathing, more lightness in the body, greater serenity in the spirit; pleasures are less ardent there, passions more moderate. Meditations take an inexpressibly grand and sublime character in proportion to the objects that impress us, a tranquil voluptuousness that has nothing to do with anything harsh or sensual. It seems that in rising above the dwellings of men, one leaves behind all low and earthly sentiments, and to the degree that one approaches the ethereal regions, the soul acquires something of their inalterable purity.

Rousseau views mountains as an earthly paradise where one can be healed and transformed, both physically and spiritually. He even sees them as a sublime site of mystical transcendence in which the soul loses itself in an experience of the divine:

Imagine the variety, the grandeur, the beauty of a thousand astonishing sights.…In the end the spectacle has something—I don't know what—of magic, of the supernatural, that ravishes the spirit and the senses; one forgets everything, one forgets oneself, one no longer knows where one is.

Until the 18th century locals knew Mont Blanc, highest peak in the Alps, as Mont Maudit, the "Accursed Mountain." With the rise of the Enlightenment and romanticism, the Alps lost demonic association and the mountain was renamed Mont Blanc, the "White Mountain." The impressions of the poet and philosopher Johann Wolfgang van Goethe on first seeing Mont Blanc reflect this change:

> *The stars came out one by one, and we noticed above the summits of the mountains before us a light we could not explain. It was clear, without brilliance, like the Milky Way, but more dense, a bit like the Pleiades, only more extensive. The sight of it riveted our attention.... A pyramid illuminated by a mysterious, inner light... appeared to soar above the summits of all the mountains; and we knew that it could only be the summit of Mont Blanc.*

The sight of its summit evokes a sense of the sublime.

With the full development of romanticism in the early 19th century, the Alps became expressions of the infinite itself. The English poet Percy Bysshe Shelley wrote a poem titled "Mont Blanc: Lines Written in the Vale of Chamouni" in which he addresses the mountain as an embodiment of divine power:

> *Thou hast a voice, great Mountain, to repeal*
> *Large codes of fraud and woe; not understood*
> *By all, but which the wise, and great, and good*
> *Interpret, or make felt, or deeply feel.*
> *Mont Blanc yet gleams on high: — the power is there,*
> *The still and solemn power of many sights,*
> *And many sounds, and much of life and death.*
> *... The secret Strength of things*

Which governs thought, and to the infinite dome
Of Heaven is as a law, inhabits thee!

William Butler Yeats, one of the greatest poets of the 20th century, was drawn to the mystical dimension of mountains. His poem "Meru," completed in 1935, uses the image of hermits "caverned in night under the drifted snow" on Mount Meru, the mythical mountain at the center of the Buddhist and Hindu universe, to express a profound disillusionment with the accomplishments of civilization.

For all its apparent bleakness, the poem has positive implications. Around the time he composed "Meru," Yeats wrote an introduction to a Hindu swami's account of a pilgrimage to Mount Kailas, the sacred peak in Tibet regarded as the physical manifestation of Mount Meru. In it, Yeats discusses the significance of the mountain as a cosmic center and uses the same image of a cave on Meru to describe those who go beyond illusion—"man's glory and his monuments"—to attain the supreme goal of spiritual liberation:

> *He that moves towards the full moon [taking the path to liberation] may, if wise, go to the Gods (expressed or symbolized in the senses) and share their long lives, or if to Brahma's question—"Who are you?" he can answer "Yourself," pass out of these three penitential circles, that of common men, that of gifted men, that of the Gods, and find some cavern upon Meru, and so pass out of all life.*

The desolation of which the poem speaks refers to the destruction of "manifold illusion" and reveals the underlying reality that is man's ultimate salvation.

Probably inspired by his interest in Kailas and Meru, Yeats asked to join a group of England's leading climbers on their annual outing to Snowdon in Wales. Geoffrey Winthrop Young, the leader of the party, turned him down. He had heard that Yeats planned to project himself mystically up the rock in the form of a small green jade elephant. Such a person, Young felt, would be too dangerous to have as a climbing partner.

The account of the frozen body of a leopard discovered near the summit of Kilimanjaro helped inspire Ernest Hemingway to write the short story "The Snows of Kilimanjaro" and make the volcano one of the most famous mountains in modern literature. Hemingway begins with the enigmatic question this discovery poses:

> *Close to the western summit there is the dried and frozen carcass of a leopard. No one has explained what the leopard was seeking at that altitude.*

The end of the story gives a strong hint of what the leopard— and Hemingway—were seeking. The hero, a writer named Harry, lies in his safari tent, dying of gangrene. Slowly he slips into a delirium and has a vision. A bush pilot comes to rescue him, and they take off into a storm. When they come out of the clouds, Harry realizes that he is going to his death:

> *Compie [Compton, the pilot] turned his head and grinned and pointed and there, ahead, all he could see, as wide as all the world, great, high, and unbelievably white in the sun, was the square top of Kilimanjaro. And then he knew that there was where he was going.*

For Hemingway, as for the Africans themselves, Kilimanjaro was an awe-inspiring place of the dead and a symbol of the mystery into which they vanish.

The beauty of mountain views makes them natural subjects for works of art. Accomplished artists draw on the associations that mountains have in different cultures to transform our perceptions of the world around us. In the hands of a master, a mountain landscape does more than portray a beautiful scene; it evokes visions of a reality more intense and meaningful than the one of our everyday experience. We see everything in a brighter light—one that reveals aspects of the world and ourselves that we have overlooked or ignored.

The Chinese expression for landscapes and landscape paintings—*shan-shui*, or mountain-water—highlights the importance of mountains, or *shan*, in Chinese thought as one of the two basic constituents of the natural environment. The second element, *shui*, or water, takes the form of streams and rivers that spring from the heights of peaks to flow through valleys. Together the two give rise to nature as a whole and reveal the presence of the Tao, the spiritual essence of all things.

The Chinese art of landscape painting reached a peak during the northern and southern Sung dynasties. One of the classics of this period is "Early Spring," painted by Guo Xi in 1072. The fluid nature of the landscape depicted in "Early Spring," with mountains taking the shapes of clouds to drift in and out of the mist, expresses the elusive flow of the Tao—giving rise to all things, yet bound by none of them. Nothing remains fixed, everything is in flux, turning into something else and pointing to a reality beyond form, deeply mysterious and immensely attractive. "Early Spring" invites us to enter the world it depicts and lose ourselves in it, wandering forever through mountains without end.

The author of the most influential treatise on Chinese land-scape painting, Guo Xi, expresses a key reason why the Chinese people have valued the art of depicting mountain landscapes:

The din of the dusty world and the locked-in-ness of human habitations are what human nature habitually abhors: while, on the contrary, haze, mist, and the haunting spirits of the mountains are what human nature seeks, and yet can rarely find.... Having no access to the landscapes, the lover of forest and stream, the friend of mist and haze, enjoys them only in his dreams. How delight-ful then to have a landscape painted by a skilled hand! Without leaving the room, at once, he finds himself among the streams and ravines; the cries of the birds and monkeys are faintly audible to his senses; light on the hills and reflection on the water, glittering, dazzle his eyes. Does not such a scene satisfy his mind and captivate his heart? That is why the world values the true significance of the painting of mountains.

One of the greatest masters of Japanese art, Katsushika Hoku-sai, focused his attention on the inspiring form of Mount Fuji. Between 1826 and 1833, he depicted the mountain in the *Thirty-Six Views of Mount Fuji*. In many of the block prints that form this collection, the mountain stands as a symbol of stability set above and amid the turmoil of human life. Nowhere in the *Thirty-Six Views* does Hokusai evoke this vision of reality more dramatically than in the "Great Wave off Kanagawa."

In this dramatic print, an enormous breaker rears up over boats caught in surging waves. Shreds of foam reach out like fingers toward the small image of Fuji, viewed through the hollow of the breaking wave. Although the water seems about to obliterate the mountain, Fuji remains calm and serene. The furious power of the wave catches the viewer's eye and guides it to the unshakable peak. The two work together, the wild motion of the one accentuating the quiet stillness of the other.

Japanese Buddhists like Hokusai would see in the curling wave about to overwhelm the terrified people a clear reference to *samsara*, the turbulent round of life and death, and in the still point of Fuji at the center a symbol of nirvana, the serene state of freedom from fear and suffering. Just as the mountain appears within the curve of the breaker, so the experience of reality that leads to the Buddhist goal of liberation is to be found in the world of illusion. The intimate relation of wave and peak points to the realization that for all their apparent differences samsara and nirvana are one and the same, if we can see them for what they truly are: two ways of experiencing the ultimate emptiness of all things, one binding, the other liberating.

As Hokusai had done with Fuji, Paul Cézanne painted numerous views of a single mountain—Mont-Sainte-Victoire in southern France. In the 1880s, after a series of artistic rejections and personal disappointments, he withdrew to his native Aix-en-Provence and devoted himself entirely to art. There, Cézanne turned repeatedly to Mont-Sainte-Victoire, seeking to extract from its enduring limestone something fixed and eternal that would protect him from the vicissitudes of time and emotional turmoil.

An observer of Cézanne at work described his painting as a meditation with a paintbrush. As Cézanne himself explained, "The mind of the artist must be like a sensitive plate, a simple receiver at the moment he works, but to prepare the plate and make it sensitive, repeated immersions are needed—long work, meditation, study, sorrow, joy, life." He approached the act of painting a tree or mountain as a mystic would the visualization of a deity: "If I experience the slightest distraction, the slightest lapse, above all if I interpret too much, if a theory takes me out of my concentration, if I think while I am painting, if I intervene, then everything collapses and all is lost." The result of his meditation was a kind of mystical experience of unity with the object of his brush. Out of this kind of experience comes the peculiar intensity of his paintings of Mont- Sainte-Victoire.

*

MOUNTAINEERS ARE DRAWN to mountains and mountain climbing for many different reasons—perhaps as many as there are climbers, if not more. Some people climb for fame and glory, to make a name for themselves, or to conquer a mountain. Others do it for sport, in response to the challenge of doing something that requires skill and effort. Still others do it to make up for feelings of inadequacy or to prove something to themselves and others. Many go to mountains for the sense of openness and freedom they experience on the heights or to feel closer to the beauty and mystery of nature. Hidden beneath many of these reasons for climbing—sometimes conscious, sometimes not—is often a spiritual impulse that goes back at least as far as the origins of modern mountaineering in the Alps.

The transformation of European attitudes toward mountains, in which they became symbols of the sublime and the infinite, coincided with the birth of the modern sport of Alpinism—the first ascent of Mont Blanc in 1786. Horace Bénédict de Saussure, the Swiss scientist who offered a prize for this achievement and who is regarded as the father of Alpinism, was drawn to climb the mountain by the feelings of wonder and awe that moved Goethe and Shelley to write about it. He wrote the following words describing his experience high on the glaciers of Mont Blanc:

> *These fields of snow and cliffs of ice, too dazzling to be looked at in the day, what a wondrous and enchanting spectacle they present under the soft beams of the torch of night!.... Was ever such a moment given for meditation? What pains and hardships are not paid in full by moments such as these! The soul of man is lifted up, a wider, nobler horizon is offered to his view; surrounded by such silent majesty he seems to hear the very voice of Nature, and to become her confidant, to whom she tells the most secret of her operations.*

Mont Blanc continued to provide mountaineers with spiritual inspiration; George Mallory wrote about his ascent of Mont Blanc in the early 20th century:

> *Have we vanquished an enemy? None but ourselves. Have we gained success? That word means nothing here. Have we won a kingdom? No...and yes. We have achieved an ultimate satisfaction...fulfilled a destiny.... To struggle and to understand— never this last without the other; such is the law...*

Rather than conquer the mountain, the climber vanquishes himself, much as a sage or yogi overcomes his ego. Mallory discounts success and the kingdom he wins in its place evokes comparisons with the kingdom of heaven described in the New Testament. Finally, in Mallory's view, the struggle to reach the summit ends in a deeper understanding that leads to insight and wisdom.

When asked why he wanted to climb Mount Everest, Mallory replied with the most famous and commonly cited reason for climbing a mountain: "Because it is there." There is, I believe, in that reply a question: What is the "it" that is there? I would say that for many climbers, consciously or unconsciously, it is the experience of a deeper reality that gives meaning and vitality to their lives—something that draws them so powerfully that they are willing to risk their lives for that experience. Mallory himself vanished into the "it" that is there on Mount Everest. In 1924 he and his companion, Andrew Irvine, disappeared into the clouds near the summit.

Explaining on another occasion why he was going to Everest, Mallory reportedly said:

> *So, if you cannot understand that there is something in man which responds to the challenge of this mountain and goes out to meet it, that the struggle is the struggle of life itself upward and forever upward, then you won't see why we go. What we get from this adventure is just sheer joy. And joy is, after all, the end of life.*

The joy that he sought on the heights of Mount Everest represented for Mallory an ultimate end, his own equivalent to the bliss experienced by mystics and sages on their spiritual quests.

Many who hike and climb for sport and recreation are seeking an experience of spiritual awakening in the mountains in which their perceptions of themselves and the world around them are transformed and renewed. Maurice Herzog, the leader of the 1950 French expedition that made the first ascent of Annapurna—the first of the highest Himalayan peaks to be climbed—describes a dramatic example of such an experience as he approached the unclimbed summit:

> *This diaphanous landscape, this quintessence of purity—these were not the mountains I knew: they were the mountains of my dreams.... An astonishing happiness welled up in me, but I could not define it. Everything was so new, so utterly unprecedented.... I thought of the famous ladder of St. Theresa of Avila. Something clutched at my heart.*

A powerful experience of this kind high on a mountain may even overturn old conceptions and awaken a new awareness and appreciation of people and things back home. Herzog refers to just such a shift in attitude and the long-lasting effects it can have:

> *In my worst moments of anguish, I seemed to discover the deep significance of existence of which till then I had been unaware. I saw that it was better to be true than to be strong. The marks of the ordeal are apparent on my body. I was saved and I had won my freedom...the assurance and serenity of a man who has fulfilled himself.... A new and splendid life has opened out before me.*

Here lies perhaps the greatest reward of climbing a mountain.

Troll Wall, Norway JOHN AMATT

upward and forever upward ✳ JOHN AMATT

"Mountains symbolize the indomitable will, an unbending resolution,
a loyalty that is eternal, and character that is unimpeachable....
When man pits himself against the mountain, he taps inner
springs of his strength. He comes to know himself. For he realizes
how small a part of the universe he actually is, how great are
the forces that oppose him."

WILLIAM O. DOUGLAS

WHEN I CLIMBED MY FIRST MOUNTAIN, I was a shy, underachieving youth who aspired for success but lacked the confidence to achieve it. Vivid in my mind is a memory of a family holiday in southern England several years before that first climb. While sightseeing we had become lost. It was starting to get dark. As we came to a row of houses in a picturesque village, my father told me to get out of the car and ask someone for directions back to our hotel. I was stricken with panic. Tears welled up in my eyes. With head down and arms folded tightly across my chest, I refused to leave the car. The idea of speaking to a stranger was something that I simply could not face.

One bleak Scottish day a few years later, we hiked up the Old Pony Track on Ben Nevis, at 4,406 feet (1,343 meters) the highest mountain in the British Isles. At 11 years of age, I was soon to start a new life at a British public school, and that day I was proudly wearing my crisp uniform, replete with school cap, necktie, kneesocks, and short pants. For protection against adverse weather, I was wearing a gabardine raincoat.

As we gained height, the rain increased in intensity. Soon the wind was driving sheets of mist horizontally across the trail. I was cold, wet, and dispirited. *What's the point of this?* I thought. *It would be so much warmer back in the car parked at the trailhead.* I began to grumble about going back down.

I will never forget my father looming over me with a stern face, rain streaking his cheeks. "If you turn around now," he said, "you'll regret it for the rest of your life!"

His words were a challenge. I felt the heat of defiant anger rising inside me. *I'll show him,* I thought as I shot off up the trail with my sister, Susan. *What does he know?* With our coats pulled tight against the freezing rain, we doggedly pushed ahead. Soon we left my parents behind anxiously asking other hikers if they had seen two youngsters up ahead. When they finally reached the top, Susan and I had been there for an hour, shivering in the icy cold.

Although I didn't know it at the time, this experience would launch me on the journey of personal exploration and self-discovery. I began to follow in the footsteps of Alexander Graham Bell, an adventurous soul whose natural curiosity changed civilization through his invention of the telephone. In 1914, he offered the following advice: "Don't keep forever on the public road, going only where others have gone. Leave the beaten track occasionally and dive into the woods. You will be certain to find something you have never seen before. Of course, it will be a little thing, but do not ignore it. Follow it up, explore all around it; one discovery will lead to another, and before you know it you will have something worth thinking about to occupy your mind. All really big discoveries are the results of thought."

Having succeeded on Ben Nevis, I began to probe my strengths and my limitations, to question my previous beliefs, and to explore my potential by seeking challenges on mountains of increasing difficulty around the world.

It is possible my path was destined by another holiday my parents took before I was born. They were vacationing in Grindelwald, Switzerland, during the summer of 1938, when the Eiger North Face was climbed for the first time. As they were leaving the railway station to travel home, their guide told them, "There are four more fools on the Eiger." In fact, this was the first ascent party of Anderl Heckmair, Ludwig Vorg, Fritz Kasparek, and Heinrich Harrer, and by the time my folks arrived home the story was front-page news.

As a youngster, I spent many an hour browsing through the yellowed clippings that my dad had collected from that time. Seeking further inspiration, I devoured my father's well-worn copy of *The White Spider*, Heinrich Harrer's classic history of the Face, and dug into his collection of narratives on the early British attempts to climb Mount Everest. As I dreamed of climbing in their footsteps, I pored through the autobiographies of modern European climbing heroes, such as Walter Bonatti, Gaston Rebuffat, and Lionel Terray, enthralled by their moments of self-discovery during triumphs and tragedies on mountains around the world. And as my climbing skills grew throughout my teenage years, I met some of the greatest British mountaineers of the early 1960s, including Joe Brown, Don Whillans, Tom Patey, and Chris Bonington. Their words and deeds became my call to action.

Nine years after Ben Nevis, I found myself at the foot of another cold, wet mountainside, this time in Norway. With three friends, I was bivouacked below the soaring Troll Wall, aspiring to make the first ever ascent of this "Wall of the Giants," which is considered to be the highest vertical rock wall in Europe. It was said that a stone dropped from the summit would touch nothing until it landed in the valley 5,000 feet below. At this point in 1965, nobody had climbed, or even tried to climb, the Troll Wall. More experienced climbers had come to look, but had turned their backs and walked away. With the audacity of youth, we decided to try. And it was here that I learned the meaning of courage, which Mark Twain defined as "resistance to fear, mastery of fear—not the absence of fear."

As I sought sleep that night, my mind was a turmoil of fear and anxiety; I worried about all the things that could go wrong up on that unknown wall. But as I struggled with these doubts, I knew that unless we started the climb the next morning, we would never discover if we were up to the challenge.

My climbing companion Tony Howard caught the mood in an article for the British magazine *Mountain Craft:*

> *Once admitted, [fear] gnaws away at your subconscious; it prods and probes at every chink in your mental armor. It can mushroom into a nightmare of fear from which there is no release until dawn; the slow dawn that lights the sky with a pale golden glow, yet refuses to burst over the black horizon. You wish to hell the sun would hurry....*
>
> *...waiting, eternally waiting and thinking, second after second ticking slowly into minutes, into long, long hours. The thoughts multiply, obsess you and devour*

you. You wish you had never set foot on rock; you decide the whole venture is too big for you, and you can only sit and wait, a victim of your own weaknesses.

High on the Troll Wall, I was forced to learn how to control my fear. For eight days, we faced sleet, falling rocks, and gusts of icy wind, while inching our way up the precipice. At night, we tied ourselves onto ledges no more than a foot and a half wide and tried to sleep. Occasionally, we dozed while standing upright on tiny footholds—before our knees collapsed, jerking us awake.

On the penultimate day, I was climbing last while Tony and Bill Tweedale tackled the final set of overhangs. As they disappeared overhead, I was left alone, dangling over a sheer drop of more than 3,000 feet. Only the jerking of the rope from above signified progress.

Then all movement overhead stopped. Anxiously, I waited for the ropes to pull tight, a signal that I could continue. Minutes drifted into hours with no sound from above. My mind began to race with worst-case scenarios. Had they reached an impasse? Was one of them hurt? Would we be forced to retreat from so high on the wall? Could we, in fact, get down? The ropes were swinging free below my feet, not even touching the rock. Unable to communicate with my companions, it was all I could do to control the growing panic.

A noise from above broke through this tide of fear. The rope started to snake upward and became tight. With immense relief, adrenaline surging through my body, I started to climb.

What drives us into such situations? Why do people voluntarily seek out such discomfort and uncertainty in the mountains? And what do we learn from such exposure to the unknown that makes us better people in our everyday lives? The answer I have learned through years of climbing is this. Only when I am forced to confront adversity, often by external events beyond my control, or when I choose to struggle by seeking out a challenging new route to a mountain's summit, for example, do I find out what I am truly capable of achieving.

I have also discovered that it is not during the struggle that the learning takes place, or even when standing on the summit, having achieved the goal. The truth comes to light afterward, when I can take a step back and digest the experience. Having reflected, I can then gaze out toward many more mountains of opportunity, ready to take the next step forward in learning.

Looking back at our first ascent of Norway's Troll Wall in 1965, I realize today that the most significant part of that climb was our willingness to try, to commit to an effort that others had rejected, and to find the courage to begin. During that sleepless night at the foot of the climb, I began to appreciate that when you look fear directly in the face, it recedes in front of you; when you run away from fear, it only grows in your mind. I began to think of fear and anxiety as simply being nature's way of keeping us focused on the task at hand. Once I understood that fact and made the decision to start the climb, all the other pieces quickly fell into place.

By every measure, our Troll Wall experience symbolized the very essence of adventure. It was a true journey into the unknown; no one had been up that mountain face before. If we had gotten into trouble, there were few that could have come to our aid, given the extreme nature of the climbing and the remoteness of the location. But at the time I was exactly where I wanted to be. And it was this success on the Troll Wall that opened my personal realm of possibility, which years later would take me to Nepal as a member of the first Canadian team ever to try to climb the world's highest peak.

The Canadian Mount Everest Expedition in the fall of 1982 was a controversial project from the start: a traditional-style, large-team effort with major corporate support and extensive media coverage. With a nationalistic agenda, the objective was to place a Canadian on top of the mountain for the first time.

Departing Kathmandu, we embarked on a three-week walk to the foot of the mountain, establishing Base Camp toward the end of the monsoon rains. We had decided to take an entirely new route, via the South Pillar. Two weeks into the climb, we had established the route through the tortuous Khumbu Icefall and moved on into the Western Cwm. Everything was going well when our effort was decimated by two tragic accidents in which four people died. Seven climbers were buried in an avalanche that fell hundreds of feet from the West Shoulder of Everest. Three Sherpas moving together along the fixed ropes were killed. Then, two days later, cameraman Blair Griffiths perished in a collapse in the Icefall. In both cases, we had been in the wrong place at the wrong time.

Looking back, I believe that, prior to the accidents, we had started to feel too certain of our success. Because everything was proceeding as planned, we were already feeling assured of the achievement to come. We were looking toward the summit with tunnel vision, when we should have had peripheral vision. We should have been checking around every day and adapting our approach to the changing conditions on the mountain. Without realizing it, we had fallen into complacency—the greatest danger in extreme situations. We were implementing a plan that had been developed in the comfort of our homes in Canada—a plan that was based upon a series of assumptions as to what it would be like on Everest, half the world away. On arriving at the mountain, we had not checked, and kept checking, to see if these assumptions were correct.

In the face of these tragic events, our reaction was to place blame. When something goes wrong, we have to have a reason; something must have been at fault. We were blaming ourselves, thinking that if we hadn't been so selfish as to want to climb this mountain, these men would still be alive. But the Sherpas viewed the deaths from a different perspective. Being Buddhist, they believed in karma and reincarnation. They came to us saying, "This was meant to be. If these men hadn't died on Everest today, they would have died somewhere else today, because this was their day to journey on into their next life." Rather than place blame, they encouraged continuing the climb.

Truly, the accidents on Everest were beyond our control. Nobody could have predicted the second when an avalanche would fall from hundreds of feet above our heads. Neither could we know exactly when a collapse would occur in the Icefall. It could be said at the time of the tragedies that we had failed. But by reflecting on what had happened and adapting our plan, we knew we still had a chance to complete the climb. The tragedies had burst our bubble of invincibility, and brought focus to our effort.

Lucien Devies, president of the Himalayan Committee of the Federation Française de la Montagne, writes in heroic terms of the struggle for the summit in his preface to Maurice Herzog's *Annapurna: The First 8,000 metre Peak*: "Man overcomes himself, affirms himself, and realizes himself in the struggle towards the summit, toward the absolute. In the extreme tension of the struggle, on the frontier of death, the universe disappears and drops away beneath us. Space, time, fear, suffering, no longer exist. Everything then becomes quite simple. As on the crest of a wave, or in the heart of a cyclone, we are strangely calm—not the calm of emptiness, but the heart of action itself. Then we know with absolute certainty that there is something indestructible in us, against which nothing shall prevail."

In the days that followed, bad weather forced all the climbers down to Base Camp, allowing for catharsis. As time healed our wounds, our desire to climb was rekindled. We would return with a smaller team, moving more quickly through the danger zones. We would abandon our hopes of climbing a new route via the South Pillar and opt instead for the easier South Col route. The summit beckoned.

Five weeks later, Laurie Skreslet, Sungdare, and Lhakpa Dorje stood on top of the world. It was so clear they could see where the horizon curved, with Kanchenjunga in the far distance and Makalu and Lhotse closer at hand.

Two days later, Pat Morrow, Pema Dorje, and Lhakpa Tshering followed. On the summit that day, the temperature was minus 40°F, so cold that the batteries could not charge Pat's camera, prohibiting him from exposing his film correctly to the light. Removing his mitts, he was forced to manually operate the camera, taking multiple shots of the same view, each with a different exposure. By bracketing several exposures, he would strive for one, and only one, perfect image.

Now a renowned adventure photographer, Pat is often asked how he takes such great photographs. With considerable understatement, he answers, "F-8... and be there!" suggesting that all he has to do is ensure the film is correctly exposed to the light, and be in the right place to click the shutter. What he means is: he keeps it simple.

Eighteen months after returning from Nepal, I found myself walking across the giant stage of Radio City Music Hall in New York, the largest indoor theater in the world. As the closing speaker of the 57th Annual Meeting of the Million Dollar Round Table, a global association of life insurance agents, I had come to relate my story of Everest. Facing the 6,000 strangers in the audience, I reflected upon how I had evolved from a shy, underachieving youth that could not ask a stranger for directions to a man who could now speak to thousands. Such is the growth gained through the willingness to explore extreme landscapes.

Howser Towers, Bugaboos, British Columbia PIERRE LEMIRE

the landscapes within us ✳ BERNARD AMY

All Nature is a pillared temple where,
At times, live columns mutter words unclear;
Forests of symbols watch Man pass, and peer
With intimate glance and a familiar air.

CHARLES BAUDELAIRE

ONE HAS ONLY TO GO from the Alps to the Himalaya or Alaska, from the Atlantic coast of France to the southern seas, from the forests of Europe to the American far north or the Amazonian jungle, or from Death Valley to the Sahara, to appreciate that some landscapes are more extreme than others. But are they really? Is the extreme quality of a landscape an attribute that is objective or subjective? Can it be measured? And what does it have to do with that anxious pleasure, that mixture of attraction and fear, aroused in us by the most extreme landscapes?

There are objective physical parameters that are linked to the extreme nature of a landscape. The height of a face or a mountain range; the strength of an ocean wind and the size of the waves; the temperature; an area's remoteness measured in miles—these can explain the awe inspired in us by a certain landscape. But these measurements can't explain everything. In any experience where we are confronted by nature, we realize that there is also a subjective aspect to one's perception of a landscape.

A landscape affects us because it is a symbol—it triggers a form of recognition within us, often without our realizing it, and creates associations of ideas. Because of its evocative power, a landscape can awaken in our minds other symbols that, in turn, take us back to deeply etched memories such as personal images, historic accounts, and myths.

There is nothing mysterious about this evocative power. We interpret all of the information we perceive using any means at our disposal, which includes our conscious and unconscious memory, both psychological and corporeal. Most of the information we process during the course of our lifetime has to do with objects or events so familiar that we interpret them directly using simple pattern matchings, which happen too quickly for associations of ideas to be created. But in some cases the links between the images in one's memory and other, more remote, images are strong enough to activate more distant patterns that will then modify the global interpretation of the perceived information. The perceived object thus becomes a symbol.

✳

SYMBOLIC THOUGHT PRECEDES LANGUAGE and discursive reasoning, as Mircea Eliade has noted, by conditioning our vision of the world. Images that are at a deep level, symbols, and myths meet a need and fulfill a purpose: to lay bare the most secret modalities of the soul to allow a better understanding of man—"basic man," who has not yet had to come to terms with history. And it would be illusory to believe that modern man, and modern Western man in particular, is not subject to these processes.

It is man's nature to apprehend the universe in a manner that is simultaneously rational and irrational, logical and sentimental, intuitive and deductive, mystical and scientific, without there being any overriding proof of the preeminence of one or the other of these attitudes, which in daily life are constantly intermingled. And modernity is not about to destroy the symbols and myths lying within the hearts of human beings; rather, it simply forces people to rethink them at a higher level of consciousness.

For lovers of extreme landscapes, symbolic processes are essential; they give the wilderness experience its richness and provide a great deal of meaning to a humanistic approach to the preservation of wilderness. It is not just a matter of leaving future generations areas in which to recreate. These areas must give them the possibility of reliving fundamental symbolic associations.

Extreme landscape is able to flush out memories and then activate them within us to the point of letting them influence our experiences. These memories are recollections of distant events that go back in time to varying extents in our own personal history, in the history of our society, and in the history of our species. And this distance in time determines what can metaphorically be called the spatial "depth" of the memory, which is linked to the level of consciousness where the memory may be found. We think of a series of spherical layers superimposed on each other, the outer layer being our immediate conscious mind. Moving inward, one eventually reaches the central kernel, our most secret unconscious. The various levels are closely linked, and the "working" zones of our memories—as they process our immediate experiences, seemingly at the surface—are more or less influenced by the most inner zones.

Any experience of landscape activates the full range of symbols, but to various degrees; the "deeper" ones are the least clearly evoked by habitual landscapes. The evocative power of the deepest images— the strength with which they are reactivated to the point of becoming almost conscious—no doubt constitutes the parameter that combines with physical criteria in order to determine the extremeness of a landscape. The more intensely it evokes experiences very distant in time, the more a landscape will seem extreme to us.

✳

THE EXPERIENCES EVOKED BY A LANDSCAPE belong to a great variety of time periods. They may belong to our fairly recent personal history. But they may also have marked our first encounters with extreme landscapes, or further back in time have belonged to our childhood and our first contacts with the world. The family garden and its mysteries constitute an initial extreme landscape that is made accessible by learning to walk but that seems enormous to the little one who is setting off to explore it. More deeply still, they may be much more distant experiences whose recollections are etched in the collective part of our memory and that date back to our species' first contacts with the world—those harshest of contacts, from before the time when man learned to soften some of his relationships with nature.

✳

As it relates to our recent past, extreme landscape has primarily symbolized the knowledge we have gained about wild nature. This knowledge tends to attenuate the extreme nature of any wilderness we confront. What we see and what we feel about the landscape tells us that it is extreme; however, the techniques we have developed to confront it and the memory of our previous experiences remind us that we know how to survive in such an environment. The extremeness of the environment is thus diminished. A classic example is our adaptation to high altitude: The oxygen pressure at altitude remains very low, as it always has been, but now we know in advance what the physical challenge is going to be, and doctors today realize that the body develops a sort of cellular memory that allows it to anticipate the necessary adaptive mechanisms.

But at the same time, a recollection subsists of the times when extreme wilderness imprinted in us, in most cases painfully, a clear awareness of our limits. And that recollection deters us from minimizing the difficulties of any adventure we embark on.

It is because of this tension between the sangfroid created by familiarity and the anxiety aroused by the recollection of failures that a given landscape will seem extreme to some people but not to others. Ultimately, when familiarity prevails completely over the ever more distant recollection of failures, then the landscape almost ceases to seem extreme. This is well known by mountain guides, who are aware of the dangers of spending too much time in the mountains, as well as by climbers, who realize that some of their most extreme feats can be the result of extreme recklessness.

✳

If one searches for what extreme landscape evokes in us, one reaches a part of our memory that for the most part escapes our control and that plays a role in the collective memory of our species. In it are imprinted traces of the crucial experiences lived by human beings during their long history. Among those experiences, three must have played a primordial role: Our species' departure from the forests and our discovery of the sky and of natural forces originally considered supernatural; the slow accession of man to the status of an upright animal gradually aware of his verticality; and, finally, the species' expansion over the entire surface of the globe through successive waves of big migrations. The increasingly unconscious memory of these three great events that initially forged the human soul has established in our minds three types of symbolism that play important roles in the interpretation of landscape: the symbolism of verticality, the symbolism of altitude, and the symbolism of distance.

In order to understand the central importance of mountains in the world's religions, the French writer Samivel took a particular interest in the first two types of symbolism: "Being man's normal posture in his active state, verticality defines a preferred direction from low to high—an opinion that is reinforced by several convergent characteristics such as a person's increase in height from childhood to adulthood and the feeling of power and security engendered by an 'elevated' position.

"As a result, verticality in itself is viewed positively and anything expanded along this axis will be valued in the same way: tall is 'better' than short because what is taller is stronger; what is higher is 'better' than what is lower.

"These judgements emanate from the depths of our primitive soul; they structure our physical space and give it positive or negative meaning, wholly influence the world of myths and are reflected in everyday metaphors such as 'small-minded' and 'to raise one's child.' "

These same value judgments lead the highest place to be considered the place of perfection, and thus make the sky the abode of gods—gods considered the masters of natural forces that are for the most part created by celestial phenomena.

The enhanced value given to verticality and the sacralization of altitude mean that any ascent is a double symbol: It is both a climb toward the gods and a vertical distancing of oneself far away from the world of men and its imperfections. Because by moving upward he places himself physically above other people, any mountaineer, whether he wants to or not, engenders more or less consciously in himself the idea that he is for a moment symbolically above his fellow human beings. When a child, who is used to having to look at adults by lifting his head, reaches the top of a climbing wall for the very first time, he finds himself lowering his head in order to see his teacher. His neck muscles transmit this motor information to his brain, the ancient symbolic processes immediately affect the interpretation of the perceived information, and the child, because he is "looking from up high," feels taller and therefore stronger than the adult, who was superior until now. The child is filled with a new confidence he has not known before.

The symbolism of distance, for its part, is linked to geographical removal, to departure and to the journey. It culminates, both physically and metaphorically, in one of the most remarkable experiences of a journey: the crossing of a pass or a ridge (passes being under the jurisdiction of the deity Janus, guardian of doorways, gates, and beginnings, whose two opposing faces simultaneously look back at what one is leaving and forward to where one is going). During the intoxicating moment of the "Gaze over the Pass"—that instant when what is imaginary is confronted by reality, when the new landscape comes to meet the landscape that has been imagined during the whole of the climb—the traveler still has time to turn around and see in the distance the area he is leaving and the human traces remaining behind. He realizes that by crossing the pass he will lose sight of these traces—in contrast to the ascender, who, though he is moving away from humans, can still see them. Nor is the anxiety of the pass crosser the same as that of the climber: A voice inside the former whispers to him that he is leaving his tribe's territory and that in so doing he is losing the safety provided by his own people.

Today, the richest possible experience, both physically and symbolically, is therefore that which combines the three types of symbolism, thus allowing us to relive all the past experiences that form the foundation, not only of our species but also of our identities as individuals. Through this experience we can each relive our earliest adventure in nature, and feel like the first human being departing to conquer the world.

The experience I am referring to is that of confronting a mountain. In order to reach a summit, one must first go toward this summit and therefore leave one's home and the safety provided by others. Then, having left, one must ascend beyond familiar territory and move up toward the celestial regions. If this is one's first ascent, one's happiness will be all the greater. The child who, for the first time, reaches the top of the mountain above his home—what the Austrians call *hausberg*—realizes full well that in order to see his parents as tiny specks far below him he first had to leave them and agree to give up their protection, venturing off into the world. He remembers that on his departure the mountain seemed not only high but also inordinately far away. The profound pleasure experienced at that moment is identical to the fascination exerted on all traveling mountaineers by the appearance of a high range of mountains at the far end of an immense plain.

The continual reenactment of this first voyage toward a summit not only creates and strengthens a personal passion; it also provides a reminder each time of the fundamental reasons that push us toward the summits. Remoteness and verticality, distance and height—one doesn't climb mountains because they are *there* but because they are *over there*. And because they rise above human beings.

Middle Sepik River, Papua New Guinea CHRIS RANIER

ancient stories, new technologies ✳ CHRIS RAINIER

I WAS TREKKING in the high forest mountains of New Guinea, heading toward the isolated tribal lands of this Stone Age island. I had been traveling for several weeks in search of peoples with one foot still planted in the Garden of Eden—to find a culture still defined by its connection to the landscape. One day, as I began to climb a steep ridge, I noticed a lone figure sitting on the top of the mountain. It took hours of toil to reach him. We smiled at one another, two beings from different moments in human history. As I paused to rest, the old man looked at me a long time, deep in thought. Finally he asked a question my guide quickly translated for me: "Which valley are you from?" I smiled. In this part of the world valleys can demarcate different worlds, and people rarely venture from one to another. Ridge tops mark the edge of a horizon. In the deep valleys and steep mountainsides of New Guinea, isolation is created by inpenetrable green walls.

The old man persisted. "Which valley are you from?" I asked my guide to let him know I came from a valley very far away. The old man's curiosity was amplified. He continued, "No, which valley are you from?" How could I begin to explain which "valley" I was from—a world so very different from the one that lay before our eyes. I politely continued with my vagueness. We continued in a gentle dialogue, then after a while, he smiled as if he was answering his own question. Slowly he spoke to my translator. "I know—you are from where the green meets the blue." He had heard of place where the color of the mountains ends and a place where the color of the sky begins.

I've thought a lot about that wise old man sitting alone on a high mountain pass wearing his rattan loin skirt, bow and arrow carefully placed beside him, and about this landscape where the green meets the blue. In New Guinea the land itself is alive, a powerful force to be embraced, respected, and honored. The powerful forces of the landscape have determined a large part of the uniqueness of the New Guinea culture, isolated from the rest of the world. If the contours of the land define whom a people are, then so their language is also defined by the land. Because the valleys have kept tribes apart, over a thousand unique languages have evolved in isolation.

A tribal nation in New Guinea is defined by a valley's edge— a border beyond which one does not journey. The four corners of the old Yali warrior's valley determines the predictable rhythms of his daily life. Just as the Tuaregs of the Sahara define their world by the waves of windblown sands of North Africa, and the nomadic existence of the Cossack reindeer herders is determined by the icy plains of northern Asia, modern man's "landscape" has been defined by the technology he has created.

As one species living on the planet, from the warrior hidden in the valley of New Guinea to the mass of humanity struggling to live out their lives in 10,000 megacities of the world's modern urbanscapes, one truth has become evident—our need to communicate among ourselves has become paramount to our survival.

Sharing stories has been a human trait since we began our search for resources across the landscape of the planet. I was reminded of this again one chilly night when I was staying with the Mek tribe of the central highlands of Irian Jaya. I had been traveling for most of the day, hiking through a moist fog, which often lingers all day in the valleys of this ancient land. I had found a village and was asked to stay with the men in their hut. As with most of the tribal groups of the island of New Guinea, the men live in one long hut, while women have their own separate hut. Children live with their mothers until they are about five; then the boys move in with the men to learn the ways of the elders. The girls stay with their mother until they are eligible to be married, which is at the time of menstruation; then a husband is picked and a special hut is built for her.

I was glad to be invited to stay the night and take a rest. Sitting around the fire that always burns in the darkened corners of the men's huts, young boys gathered to learn how to become like their older brothers, who will become warriors. Sitting taller, with an air of reserved wisdom, were the older men—the speakers of the tribal wisdom. In hushed tones and with somber looks the men talked to the boys. The young students of life sat silent, listening. The fire reflected and danced in their eyes.

The ancient tradition of storytelling involved the passing of knowledge from one generation to the next. In their potent words, the elders told the tales of the hunt, battles with their enemies, and the initiations that would soon allow the boys to pass from childhood to adulthood—the journey from youth to wisdom through the landscape of their village life. As I sat transfixed by this scene, I became aware that within this act of telling the story of life were the roots of all religions and mythologies of the human race. The need to tell the tales of life is central to the human spirit, and the desire to pass along the wisdom that lies deep in all of our souls is the catalyst for the survival of our spiritual being. These tales were profoundly influenced by the contours of this rugged and primordial landscape of green valleys. This collective story of life runs like a deep river through the human being, bringing meaning to our lives beyond daily hardships, whether it be hunting for wild boar or finding our way in the "concrete jungle."

What we have lost in the West is the relevance of telling stories to our everyday lives. What we have gained is the illusion that we have conquered nature and tamed the extreme landscape of the planet. And yet, as modern civilization stumbles into the 21st century, we can no longer assume that the last tribal peoples on the planet can simply be left alone to live their lives peacefully—that they will stay somehow untouched in their hidden landscapes. The era of the planet's innocence has passed. There are only a mere handful of untouched eddies that still linger beyond the reach of civilization. The sound of the chainsaw now pushes into the deepest reaches of the most isolated jungles of the Amazon. Uranium is mined just beyond the shadow of the mountain monasteries of Tibet. Oil is drilled from where camel caravans still tread across the sands of the African Sahara. We live on a planet where our resources are quickly dwindling and the exponential increase in population is putting horrific demands on natural resources. More now than ever before we must learn to share the stories that ensure our continued existence and harmony with the Earth. Within the myths of tribal life are messages that would enrich us if only we would listen.

Within the technology that modern man has created is a tool for all of us to share our story of humanity—the Internet. Within the last several years the Internet has spread its web around the planet in an intense and magical weave of communication. Before long, a Buddhist monk in Nepal, after his morning prayers, and before the morning light has touched his computer, will be able to e-mail his shaman friend, the Coptic priest living in the highlands of Ethiopia. And why not—we are all together on this planet eager to tell the story of life. The Internet has the ability to link us in a virtual "fireside chat," in which we all gather around to listen and to be heard. While the argument that this new form of world communication will even further divide the planet into haves and have-nots, the evidence is rather pointing in a different direction. The fastest-growing sector of the Internet is in developing countries. Indigenous language websites have been growing exponentially. First World language teaching programs archived on the Web have sprung to life from the Maori of New Zealand, to the Masai of Kenya, to the Navajo Nation of the Southwest desert of the United States. The power of the Internet, and its ability to democratize and invigorate communication, is spreading ever farther.

If language is the heartbeat of a culture, then it is imperative that we all help save the languages and stories of all cultures. Language survives through the desire to maintain the language and the ability to share it with others. What is unfolding from the words disseminated on the Internet is a sharing of our common human language within the diversity of unique tongues. And people are beginning to listen. Across the planet generations of tribal people have been forced into poverty and spiritual decay, their ways and ancient traditions ruptured by colonial powers. Transplanted from their spiritual homelands to overcrowded cities, tribal cultures abandon their mother tongue and the stories that kept the mythology of who they were and where they came from alive.

In Thailand, I came across a group of young monks wrapped in saffron-colored cloths, their heads shaved. They had taken their vows of faith. I spent the morning photographing them as they learned the ways of the Buddhist teacher, sharing the ancient act of falling into trance and tattooing their bodies with the invisible oil of white magic. Later that evening, I visited with them, caught in a different kind of trance—that of the powers of the Internet at the local cybercafé. Faces aglow in the blue light of the computer screen, they were excitedly passing along the sacred teachings of their master to other Buddhists. Here was the meeting of ancient culture with modern technology, a weave of two very different threads entwined together at this moment of human evolution that will draw us into a powerful new way of thinking. For those young monks, the computer was merely a new tool to speak of ancient things. Entire cities of satellite dishes have sprung up from Marrakech to Phnom Penh to Kabul. What has begun to happen is not necessarily a diluting of culture, but rather an empowering of communities to share their stories and traditions with people with similar messages. As their landscape has changed from purely physical and spiritual to the digital, a new landscape of knowledge arrives with a global perspective. The ancient landscape defined by trade routes, jungles, and hunting grounds now is becoming layered with a digital landscape of information. The ability to share their diversity as well their common links has arrived.

Tribal villages are using the Internet to empower their community by sharing their stories with people beyond their imagination. In northern Cambodia is a village known for a particular indigenous craft. Reduced over time to poverty, the village elders knew that craftsmen would have to give up their art and move to the city to make money. With that move would come the inevitable decay of community and of knowledge of the old ways. With help from a nongovernmental aid organization, the community set up a website of their crafts and soon began to sell their unique art around the globe. Within several years the community flourished, building a community center and a school that teaches their native language and art to future generations.

Along the Urumbamba Valley in the shadow of the great mountains of Peru, Quechua Indians have long been the keepers of an 2,000-year-old Andean tradition of weaving. Today, still dressed in blood-red woven dresses and circular hats, the women and young girls can be found on the Internet selling their wares and maintaining the fabric of their culture through the weaving of their cloth and the tapestry of their language. They believe by selling their fabrics created within the rich tradition of the ancient materials and patterns, they will help preserve their Incan identity. It is said that Peruvian textiles honor the Mother Earth goddess, Pachamama. Like their ancestors who came before them, they honor the land of their ancestors—and feel the bond they have with the mountains. The Quechua believe their fabrics are ambassadors for their culture, and every being in the community has the responsibility to contribute to the richness of the world.

The Kuna Indians of Panama live in tranquil beauty on a series of turquoise-bathed islands scattered along some 300 miles of the Panama coast. The Kuna have fought long and hard to preserve their paradise for future generations. They believe their society comes from the interwoven relationship between land and sea. With the introduction of the Internet, the Kuna have become advocates for environmental issues for indigenous peoples around the planet. They have helped set up programs for other tribal groups to be more aware of their biodiversity, environment, and land rights. Kuna spokesmen have traveled the globe as far away as New Zealand. They have met with Maori elders to discuss the rekindling of their culture and invigoration of a worldwide renaissance in tribal customs, promoted and facilitated by the ability to communicate via the Internet. More and more indigenous groups are linking up to the Internet and empowering themselves with the ability to tap into an ever growing well of knowledge and communication with first nations around the planet. With the ability to communicate comes the awareness of information and knowledge. From knowledge comes power—the power to control their destiny through the stories they share.

In its finest form, the Web can create electronic pathways to awareness, wisdom, understanding, and compassion. From the dawn of the human species man has worked to refine his ability to communicate. A new, profound means of dialogue has arrived. It is wise to remember technology is not a solution, merely an opportunity to improve what already exists. We still all need to work toward improving the quality of life for all humans, and the new technology of communication is only one of many ways to embrace that goal. Mankind has always had an integral relationship with the landscape that envelops him. How he finds sustenance from the land—where his spirit world dwells—and where he wanders and pauses to find spiritual enrichment is defined acutely by his landscape. This relationship to the land makes up who he is and the stories of his creation. It is only by sharing the ancient stories that we create new ones in a world forever changed by technology.

I have spent a lifetime traveling the world, seeking the mysteries of all seven continents. Several years ago I was hiking across the great Kenyan savanna of Serengeti. My wife and I spent five days wandering the golden grasslands with our Masai guide, Jackson. He spoke English, having attended a Kenyan school, and felt comfortable navigating between his world of the African bush and that of the Western world. After wondrous nights of sleeping under the African stars, with the crisp light of dawn we would go walking in search of wildlife. The two of us and Jackson, armed with his Masai spear, would walk in silence as we stepped past herds of zebra, wildebeest, and giraffe. Occasionally we would come across a pride of lions. The Masai are proud people, and have learned the ways of the African wilderness. As a rite of passage, every Masai boy must hunt down a lion armed only with a spear and his nerve. Jackson, clothed in the traditional red wrap of a Masai male, had already experienced this rite of passage— and was eager to show us his prowess as a true Masai warrior. We came closer to the lions, quietly inching forward. My heart beat with excitement and fear. What was I doing here without the protection of a vehicle or even a rifle, for that matter? Jackson's calmness helped to instill a little peace within me.

As we crouched down low in the golden grass, the lions, less than a hundred yards away, were very much aware of us. Sitting a short distance from the rest of the group was a beautiful lioness, her mane reflecting a rich adobe color in the powerful African sun. Jackson whispered to us to stay where we were. He was about to show us how lions feared him. He smiled and stood up, tall and proud in his red cloth—hesitating for a second, then beginning to sprint toward the lioness, spear in hand. The lioness noticed Jackson as he quickly approached. She stood up, her senses acutely attuned to the moment. Both man and beast stared at each other, assessing the danger. In a moment of pure poetry, as our guide rushed toward her, the lioness suddenly put her tail between her legs, turned, and ran away. Jackson continued the chase for a short while, as if to truly prove the point, then stopped. He lingered for a moment savoring the victory and then walked back to us. As he approached, sweat glistening on his dark skin, he smiled with immense pride and stated with dignity that spoke deeply of him and his people, "I am Masai. I am a warrior."

Later, as we gathered around a campfire for our last evening in the coolness of the Serengeti, we could hear the crackling of the blaze and the distant calls of hyenas. Chanda and I had come to this primordial land to feel one of the last places on the planet where wildlife roamed as it had done for millennia on the African continent. Along the way we had become entranced by the beauty and strength of the Masai people. Within the simplicity of their daily lives they incorporated the rhythms of land, sky, and the animals they lived among. After a lull in the conversation, Jackson said, "I have answered so many questions about my people and this place. Can I ask you some questions?" He took a moment pondering where he was going with his questions, then he spoke. "I want to know in your land, what are your initiation rituals? …What do you do with your elders when they get old?…And what do you do with your land to preserve it for the children and their children to come?" I paused to think carefully about what he was asking. I found I could not come up with an adequate answer that defined my modern culture. In the end he was most excited about the possibility of meeting with a Navajo Indian elder from the Southwest desert of America. He wanted to talk to him about how his people looked after their pastoral land—preparing it for the seventh generation.

Since man took his first steps across the extreme African landscape all around me that night, he has created stories to be told, and tales to be heard. And now in the first moments of the 21st century, Jackson will be able to easily talk to the Navajo elder and share in the common rituals that tie us together. Jackson will possibly share his view of the Serengeti as a place to tend his cows and how he became a warrior after his meeting with the great lion spirit. New technology does not have to eliminate old traditions, but rather can create the opportunity to enhance traditional ways of life. Just as Jackson has been profoundly affected by the landscape of the savanna of East Africa, so too will he be affected by the technological landscape of the Internet. The electronic web of information will allow him to understand his culture better by sharing it with the world. Ancient cultures of the future will live in a landscape both physical and virtual—where the contours of digital information will be as profound as the smell of the early rains on the plains of Serengeti signaling the beginning of the great migration.

AUCA MAHUEVO, PATAGONIA, ARGENTINA   H. BROOKS WALKER

patagonia dreaming ✳ RICK RIDGEWAY

FROM AN ALTITUDE OF 1,500 FEET, I could see across the desert steppelands of Patagonia to what appeared to be the town of Rio Gallegos.
I was flying with Doug Tompkins in his small Cessna 206. He had
flown the plane down from San Francisco—a trip that had taken
ten days—and by prearrangement he had picked me up in Calafate,
a small town perched above the turquoise waters of Lago Argentino.
Although Doug and I had shared climbing and sea-kayaking adventures in many corners of the world, including Patagonia, this was
the first time I had flown with him.

"Isn't that Río Gallegos over there?" I asked.

"Yeah."

The town was now nearly abeam our position, and I could make out the airport tarmac. But instead of flying directly toward it, we were following a road that took a wide bend before turning toward town, and the airport.

"We're low on gas," Doug said, answering my question before I could ask it.

I looked down at the road again. At least traffic was light and, closer to town, the road was even paved. I remembered a sign I had read above Doug's desk in his office at the San Francisco headquarters of Espirit, the sportswear company that until recently he had managed and co-owned. "Commit and then figure it out" the sign read. Over the years I had learned that it was the way Doug liked to climb mountains, descend rivers, and run his company. So it was only consistent that it would also be the way he flew his airplane.

The road turned right and so did we. I waited for the telltale sputter of the engine, but we made our lineup without incident. As we landed, the wind was blowing so hard our ground speed was hardly more than 20 or 30 miles per hour.

"See those ropes under the wings?" Doug said as we taxied down the runway. "Open your door, then hit the pavement running and work your way out on the strut. Grab the rope and hang on it so I can turn the plane. Otherwise, this wind might flip us."

The technique worked, and in a few minutes we had the plane tied down. We called a taxi to take us to the office of land records for the Province of Santa Cruz, since Doug had come to Río Gallegos to research ownership records of the ranches in the region. In the office we bent over old maps that divided Patagonia into a patchwork of huge *estancias* that in many cases had been in families for three or four generations, headed by patriarchs who had migrated from Italy or Germany or Britain. Some of these families had grown wealthy back in the era when wool was king, but now, with prices depressed and the land overgrazed, some had fallen on hard times.

Doug recognized this as an opportunity. He himself was at a crossroads, adjusting to a divorce that had resulted in the sale of his half of Espirit. At first he had been disappointed. Then he began to imagine using some of the money to buy land on both the Chilean and Argentine sides of the southern cone of South America. Of all the places in the world he had traveled, he felt most connected to Patagonia. He loved the raw granite spires, the wind, the parrots, flamingoes, and rheas against the backdrop of glaciers, the Argentine gauchos and Chilean *huasos* with their beret caps and neck scarves and campfire *asados* of roasted lamb. Not that Doug wanted to buy land to become a ranch baron; rather, he wanted to turn the estancias into preserves and parks, keeping the gauchos on as caretakers and wardens. He was also thinking big, as in hundreds of thousands of acres.

✳

Doug had first visited Patagonia in 1961. Back then he owned The North Face, a company he had started as a retail store on Columbus Avenue in San Francisco, two blocks from the bohemian City Lights bookstore and next door to the Condor Club, the most famous strip joint in the city. The North Face was part of the scene in the North Beach: Carol Doda, the owner of the Condor, coming over to the store to talk to anyone who would listen to her complaints about the girls that worked for her; Janis Joplin stopping by in her Porsche because she liked to hang out with the climbers, who in those days were mostly social misfits.

One of those climbers was a 22-year-old from Maine whose parents were of French-Canadian descent. He had moved to Burbank and since been drafted into the Army and stationed in San Francisco. Yvon Chouinard's interest in climbing was rooted in an earlier interest in falconry, where he had learned to rappel cliffs to access the aeries of nesting birds of prey. Yvon hated the Army and took every opportunity to go climbing. Doug would call the sergeant in charge of Yvon's unit and yell into the phone, "Sergeant So-and-So, this is General So-and-So. I need Private Chouinard to do some yard work for me. Get him a pass and get him to the gate, on the double."

Doug, on his motorcycle, would pick Yvon up and head off to Yosemite. After he was discharged from the Army, Yvon moved to Ventura, a beach town in southern California, where he could be close to his other passion, surfing. There he set up a blacksmith's shop to make gear for climbers: pitons, carabiners, ice axes. When the surf was up, the shop was closed.

In 1968, Yvon and Doug and two other friends packed a Ford van with climbing gear, skis, and surfboards, and drove from California to Patagonia. It took six months, and at the end of the journey, they made the third ascent of Fitz Roy. For both Doug and Yvon, however, it was not only the sawtooth silhouette of the Andean skyline that attracted them. From its grass steppelands to its turquoise lakes to its beech forests, from wind-driven rain on one side of the mountain crest to desert aridity on the other, the Patagonian landscape had a wild rawness they hadn't felt any other place. In the next few years Doug and Yvon returned again and again to fish, to climb, or just to be there.

For both Doug and Yvon, Patagonia was a frontier that seemed a good match for their disdain of authority. Apart from this shared individualism, they had another common aspect to their personal histories: a lack of education. They both had barely finished high school. As young men, higher education meant rock climbing. Like most people drawn to the sport in those days, the appeal wasn't so much in taking risks as in controlling them: It was a Zen-like exercise that required a degree of self-reliance that was almost anarchical.

Risk taking, self-reliance, and self-confidence are traits common to most entrepreneurs, and Doug and Yvon are both successful businessmen. Doug built The North Face from a retail store into a manufacturer of tents, sleeping bags, and packs. In the late 1960s, his wife developed a line of dresses called Plain Jane and, sensing a potentially lucrative combination of volume and margin, Doug sold The North Face, joined his wife's operation, and changed the name to Espirit. Yvon had also expanded his climbing hardware business to include pants, shorts, shirts, and anoraks designed for alpinists. By then I was visiting him regularly in Ventura to go surfing. One day when we were driving to the beach, he said, "I'm thinking of focusing more on the clothes and less on the hardware. I mean, how many people in the world need pitons compared to the number that need a pair of well-made pants?"

That was in the early 1970s, and Yvon's idea was to make the clothes the same way he made his climbing tools, where function drove design and the goal was strength through simplicity. Searching for a name, he thought of his favorite landscape in the world, a place that conjured up the same sense of ruggedness he wanted to bring to his clothes: Patagonia.

※

I HAVE LONG BELIEVED that by the time we are young adults, most of our bedrock beliefs—the ones we use to make our choices and therefore to direct our lives—are well formed. Following that logic, I also believe that the landscapes we select to place ourselves in don't change who we are as much as we sometimes think. Rather, we tend to select the landscapes that best match who we already are.

Like Doug and Yvon, I had also been drawn to Patagonia. I had first seen the region in 1983 when flying in an old DC-3 to Antarctica; we had passed, on a rare day with no clouds, the fabled rock towers of the Torres del Paine. Our pilot banked the plane between the spires, and for a heart-stopping 60 seconds, all we could see out all the ports along both sides of the plane were walls of gray granite.

Other journeys to the region followed, and in 1991 I jumped at the chance to join Doug in his small plane as he visited estancias looking for properties to purchase. By good luck, his visit coincided with a retreat Yvon was having with the key managers of his company at an estancia nearby. When Doug finished his research in Río Gallegos, we flew the Cessna to Calafate, planning to pick up Yvon and fly north to investigate a region at the base of a massive ice-encrusted peak called San Lorenzo. In the office of land records we had learned that the government of Argentina owned this mountain as well as the land on its flanks, but that the adjacent valleys were privately held. When we pointed out the extent of the government's holdings to the official who was helping us, he was surprised. Doug told me that the surveys in some of Patagonia's more remote regions were vague at best, and similar, perhaps, to what the parcel boundaries of the American West must have been like more than a hundred years before.

The next morning Yvon, Doug, and I took off in the Cessna, flying north over the mountains. As we approached Fitz Roy, we hit the storied winds of Patagonia, winds that had crossed the southern ocean uninterrupted for 5,000 miles, then slammed against the narrow but sharp backbone of the Andes and squeezed into accelerating gusts that pummeled our small aircraft.

"Hang on, boys," Doug said. "It's getting bumpy."

Doug wanted to circle Fitz Roy for a close look. I tried to take a photograph, setting the shutter speed at 1/1000 of a second, but the plane pitched so hard the camera hit my head, cutting my eyebrow.

"I had a good look at this thing when we climbed it," Yvon yelled. "I don't need another one now."

Doug ignored Yvon and circled closer to the spire, but another gust blew us into a 30° pitch.

"Maybe today's not the day," Doug said with a grin. We retreated downwind and, once distanced from the worst of the turbulence, continued north another hour until we saw, looming ahead, the ice-encrusted crest of San Lorenzo. With its sweeping faces of fluted snow protected by cliffs of cleaving seracs, it is the most Himalayan-like mountain in Patagonia.

"Look at that southeast face," Doug said. "Nine thousand vertical feet, and it's unclimbed."

A few miles from the base of the peak we could see a ranch house and outbuildings. We descended in a spiral over the buildings until someone came out and looked up. We waved and then flew a half-mile farther to a nearby grass landing strip. In a few minutes a pickup arrived, and Rene Negro, co-owner of the estancia, stepped out of the cab and introduced himself. He invited us to the house, which had a sign next to the kitchen door that read, "You don't have to be crazy to live in Patagonia, but it helps." His wife, as delighted as he was to have visitors dropping in out of the sky, served us lunch. Afterward, Doug asked Rene if we could hike to the back of the estancia, under the southeast face of San Lorenzo. Rene opened his arms and said, "Of course."

The hike took three days. The first night we stayed up late around a fire in front of our tent, drinking wine and sharing stories from past adventures. The second night we stayed with an old gaucho who slaughtered a lamb and splayed it on a long skewer that he drove into the ground at an angle over the open fire inside his small hut. With the long knife he kept sheathed on one side of his belt, he carved and served us slices of meat sprinkled with *chimichuri* sauce from a flask he carried on the other side. We shared another bottle of our wine. The old gaucho worked for Rene, tending sheep along the back border of the estancia. He was the only person living in the area for miles in any direction, and he kept grinning and shaking his head over his good fortune of having unexpected company.

The next day, we followed a lateral moraine, hiking through groves of stunted beech to an overlook with a stunning prospect of the southeast face of San Lorenzo.

"Look, the route goes right up that face there, see?" Doug said. "We could turn that rock band on the left, then back right, then follow that gully to the summit."

There was also a cleaved serac that hung over the ice face and signs of avalanche debris at the base. Yvon and I had been caught in an avalanche in the Himalaya ten years before, and it had been a miracle that either of us survived.

"I don't know, it doesn't look too safe," I said.

"It's a lot bigger than it looks," Yvon added.

Undaunted, Doug said we should come back next year and give it a try. We hiked back to the ranch house, said good-bye to Rene, then flew north to a small town where Doug landed to drop

Yvon and me off. He was flying back to Calafate to begin talking with Rene's brother, co-owner of the estancia, about the possibility of buying El Rincon, and Yvon and I were continuing north to go fishing.

After Doug took off, Yvon and I walked across the border into Chile and caught a ferry across Lago General Carrera, a huge lake whose azure beauty is undiminished by its name. We huddled in the bow with 20 Chileans, including several children, as tornado-like williwaws blew spindrift across the deck. At mid-passage the waves were substantial, and whenever the bow caught one, sending a sheet of ice water over the passengers, all of them cheered and laughed. I thought of how, in a similar situation in America, mothers would be panicking, protecting their children, and vowing to sue the ferry company. In Patagonia, the mothers were teaching their kids to make a game of it.

On the north side, Yvon and I hitched a ride in the back of a dump truck with a dozen Chilean vagabonds. We had the driver let us off at a promising trout stream. That evening Yvon showed me how to cook fish directly on the coals of our campfire. We ate the fish on planks of tree bark. We spread our bags under the stars, and, before falling asleep, I told Yvon it had been a good day.

Yvon and I hitchhiked and fished for another week before returning home. Doug stayed down for several more weeks, scouting more properties. He found another one farther north, at the end of a deep fjord carpeted with a thick temperate rain forest. When he returned to the States, he called us and said he had made an offer on El Rincon, and was optimistic he would get it.

"Next year's the time to go back and get that east face of San Lorenzo," he said. "We're not getting any younger."

MY FIRST CLIMBING TRIP with Yvon and Doug to Patagonia had been in 1988. Yvon had spotted a photograph in the environmental journal *Earthwatch*; it was of a cluster of rime-coated rock spires rising from the back of a deep channel. A little research revealed that the towers were in a labyrinth of canals, fiords, and islands just north of the Strait of Magellan, and only one climber had ever been in the area.

"We could get those collapsible kayaks you carry on planes as checked baggage," Yvon said. "Paddle in there and climb one of the spires."

The proposal was simple, but we all knew Patagonia well enough to see hardships in our crystal ball. Yvon was also about to turn 50, and I knew it was a milestone that he was thinking about. He had tendonitis in his wrists and elbows and a chronically sore neck from an earlier injury, and he had confessed he wasn't sure how many hard trips he had left in him.

In addition to the three of us, Jim Donini, a well-known climber who had made some remarkably difficult ascents in Patagonia, Alaska, and the Karakoram, joined our adventure. Rather than make the entire round trip by collapsible kayak, we decided to charter a boat for the 70-mile upwind passage to the outer canals. We would have the boat drop us off as close as possible to the spire, then, after climbing it, assemble our kayaks and return with the wind at our backs.

In Puerto Natales we made a deal with a local fisherman, then loaded our gear into the hold of a boat redolent of aged crab juice. Under a sullen sky we nosed into a wide bay as 45-knot westerlies blew spindrift in sheets over the decks. We huddled in the tiny forecabin galley, heating tea water on a cast-iron woodstove as the boat pounded into the short, steep seas.

"Hey, Fig, feels like we're on to something," Doug said to Yvon, using a nickname he'd given him in 1968, when they had made that six-month trip in the Ford van to Patagonia. For Yvon, the low point on that former trip came when he slipped and drove an ice ax into his knee and had to lie on his back for 14 days in a wet down bag inside a dim snow cave with a low ceiling. That ordeal had marked what he thought of as one of the key passages in his life, his 30th birthday. Now, exactly 20 years later, he and Doug were back in their old playground, and although Yvon didn't yet realize it, he had set himself up for a reminder that, just as adventure in extreme landscapes is the elixir of youth, it can also be the harsh mistress of age.

Two days later, the fisherman rowed us ashore one at a time in a waterlogged skiff with barely two inches of freeboard. With all of us ashore, the fishing boat disappeared into a squall marching down the fiord, and Yvon said, "Well, boys, we've cut the cord now." We pitched our tent on a narrow toehold of land along the steep-walled fiord and hoped the spire we wanted to climb was somewhere above us. Next day we noticed to windward a single hole in the clouds speeding our direction, and a few seconds later we got a glimpse of a stunning rock spire covered in fresh rime ice.

We waited ten days, and even though our altimeter twice showed a 300-foot drop in altitude—the biggest barometric change any of us had ever witnessed—the only visible shift in weather was a drop in wind speed at the base of the spire to maybe only 50 miles an hour. Doug had to be back to work at Espirit in two weeks, and we needed one week to paddle back. Realizing that in this place there was perhaps no such thing as good weather, we resolved to give it a try.

From the base of the spire we looked up to see the madcap winds driving the icy rain in looping vortices. A brief hole in the clouds revealed rock covered in fresh rime.

"It looks grim," I shouted above the roar of the wind.

Doug agreed. Yvon didn't say anything.

"I've come here to climb," Jim yelled. "Let's get in at least a couple of pitches." He started to uncoil the rope. "Anybody going with me?"

"Yeah, I'll go," Yvon yelled.

Jim started climbing. The wind was so strong the rope arced off his waist and down to Yvon's belay without touching rock. Jim finished the first pitch, brought Yvon up, and he started the second. Ice water sheeted down the rock and then blew back up in the gusts, soaking them both. Jim and Yvon completed two more pitches and disappeared into the clouds.

They had taken both ropes, so Doug and I scouted the opposite side of the spire, hoping to find a route we could climb without rope. When that failed, we returned to look for Jim and Yvon, but there was no sign of them. It was nearly dark. "Maybe they rappelled down the other side, and they're back in camp," Doug said.

In the dark we crawled through the beech thickets and boot-sucking bogs. It was after midnight when we found camp. "They're asleep," Doug said as we approached the tents. "Hey, Fig. Wake up. Fig?" There was no reply. We picked at some food, then each crawled into our own tents. Finally I fell asleep, then opened my eyes to see the yellow fabric of my tent glowing faintly. Outside I could hear Doug fumbling with a pot and starting the stove.

"Any sign of them?" I called.

"No, it's me."

"Yvon?"

"Yeah."

"Oh man, I'm glad to hear your voice."

Jim arrived, and they told us how they had reached the summit at last light, rappelled into the night, then crawled on hands and knees through the mud and dense forest undergrowth. "That's the most strung out I've been in a long time," Yvon said.

We rested a day and then had to start the long return paddle. We took a different route back, hoping to save distance by portaging from one fiord to the next. The first day a williwaw hit so hard it flipped Yvon, and he had to crawl on top of his kayak and paddle it upside down. By the time he reached shore he was hypothermic, so we built a fire and camped there. The portage took two days, backpacking the boats through undergrowth so thick we were sometimes ten feet off the ground as we wormed through the twined branches of beech and wall-like stands of cane. Reaching the opposite fiord, we reassembled the boats and, with the wind at our backs, flew down the narrow strait, turning upwind when we reached a wide bay. As night fell, we paddled as hard as we could along a tidewater cliff, struggling to find any flat place to bivouac, knowing if we missed a stroke we could be blown backward into open water and perish.

With arm and stomach muscles cramped, we made a small toehold at last light. Months later, Yvon would confess that, in the final 15 minutes of that paddle, he began to doubt he could make it. We were safe for the night, but there was no water, and it seemed a long time until dawn. The next morning we rafted our boats together so that they were more stable and let the wind blow us across the bay. The next day we reached Puerto Natales, and on the gravel beach in front of the village, the only people to greet us were two kids. I showed one of them how to push the button on my camera, and then the four of us stood next to our boats for a group portrait.

Yvon looked out across the bay. He was quiet in the way he is when he's thinking. Then he grinned in the way he does when he's content.

＊

At the beginning of that sea kayaking and climbing journey in 1988, Yvon and Doug had rendezvoused in Puerto Natales with an old friend named George Petarek, a Polish climber who for years had been living in Patagonia. George told us how the area leading into Fitz Roy had been sold to developers who had already bulldozed a grid of streets into the flats, subdividing a former sheep estancia into single-family dwelling plots and christening the town-to-be Chalten, the Tehuelche name for Fitz Roy.

"Saving this place might be the most important thing any of us could do," Yvon said, and Doug nodded in agreement. "Makes going on these adventures seem like bullshit," Yvon added with a chuckle.

Yvon and Doug were already committed environmentalists. Patagonia the company had initiated a voluntary tithing policy of giving one percent of its gross income to environmental causes, focusing its support on grassroots efforts to save wildlands and wildlife. Doug made a disciplined effort to educate himself, working through a reading list that could match any master's degree program in environmental studies. Doug then embraced deep ecology—the philosophy that rejects the notion that the natural world exists as a "resource" for human beings—and decided to commit his life and his resources to the protection of the planet's remaining wildlands. Because of his affinity for Patagonia, as well as the comparatively cheap price of land in the region, he decided to focus much of his effort there. After our reconnaissance in his small plane in 1991, Doug closed on the parcel at the back of the deep fiord a hundred miles south of Puerto Montt, sold his house in San Francisco, and moved to the farm, named Renihue after the fiord. Over the next three years he purchased several neighboring estancias until the combined area totaled over 800,000 acres.

By then he had formed the idea to take the holdings and create what would become the world's largest privately owned national park. Called Parque Pumalin, it was an effort that, from the start, was saddled with controversy. In order to keep land prices from rising, he tried to keep his initial land purchases quiet. That invited speculation that, because his holdings went from border to sea, he was trying to cut the country in half. Another rumor circulated that the project was a secret base for money laundering, another that he was creating a Jewish state, another that it was a Nazi haven.

By the mid-'90s his actual goal had become apparent to enough people that public opinion began to shift. A survey in 1997 revealed that 30 percent of the Chileans who knew about the project thought it was a good idea and another 30 percent figured it was probably okay. But in all the press, good and bad, little was said about the land itself, other than standard tribute to the giant *alerce* groves that studded the park and mention of the waterfalls that cascaded off the beech-covered walls near the road that crosses the west side. There was even less mention of Doug's personal connection with the extreme landscape he was dedicated to saving.

And it is an extreme landscape. By then I was heading down to Patagonia every other year to join Doug for climbing and hiking outings. Like its northern counterpart in Washington and British Columbia, the fiord coast of southern Chile is punctuated by a string of glaciated volcanoes. Many of them were unclimbed, not because they hadn't been attempted, but more commonly because they were guarded by forest undergrowth so dense you could be ten or fifteen feet off the ground as you crawled through labyrinths of branches and canelike *quila*. Doug told me he once finally resorted to working his boat to the top of a dense quila thicket, then got inside the boat and "paddled" across the top. On another attempt to climb one of the coastal volcanoes, he and I struggled all day crawling on hands and knees over roots and through mud, only to discover our route had inscribed a large circle.

On that day I also remember pausing in that undergrowth with Doug as he stood motionlessly watching a *chucao*, a diminutive wrenlike bird endemic to the damp rain forests of southern Chile, as it approached to within 12 inches of us. By then he was expert on the trees, and he pointed to the different species of beech, to the *ulmo*, whose white flowers, favored by bees, produce a distinct honey prized by Chileans, and, of course, to the alerces. Once flying in a remote back corner of Pumalin, we spotted a grove of alerces, and in the center a grand patriarch, a tree larger than any Doug had seen, which could have been over a thousand years old when Christ was alive. Doug has crossed and recrossed this same area dozens of times, and he has never again been able to locate the giant alerce.

On another visit we managed to push through the forest undergrowth to gain a glacier descending from one of the volcanoes along the coast. Approaching the top, we passed fumaroles of sulfur steam that had colored the seracs into shining emerald gemstones. It was a rare day with no clouds and no wind. On the virgin summit we stood in silence, looking one way across the Pacific, the other across the hundreds of thousands of acres of Parque Pumalin, a distance that extended north to the horizon.

"It's hard to believe," I said to Doug, "that as far as we can see, this place is protected, and all because a bunch of women bought a bunch of dresses."

"And the real irony," Doug said, smiling mischievously, "is that they were dresses they didn't even need."

※

KRIS McDIVITT, former CEO of Patagonia and now married to Doug, oversaw much of the management of the farm while Doug focused on the construction of the park's infrastructure: a visitors center, restaurant, lodge, trails and campgrounds, administrative buildings. The two also traveled widely through both the Chilean and Argentinean sectors of Patagonia. Doug continued acquiring wildlands whose titles were transferred to a conservation foundation he had created: a large beech forest in Tierra del Fuego threatened by a North American logging company, an entire 400,000-acre drainage on the Chilean coast, 200,000 acres of wetlands in northern Argentina that is an important flyway for migratory birds.

By the end of 2000, however, Doug could see he was approaching the limit of his foundation's ability to acquire wildlands: There were costs of maintaining and protecting what they already had. But as he and Kris continued to crisscross the region, sometimes by car, sometimes in a small two-seat Husky, they found more areas that needed protection, areas that could be purchased for 30 or 40 dollars an acre. There were two parcels totaling 225,000 acres on the Atlantic coast just north of the Strait of Magellan, with huge penguin and seal rookeries vulnerable to nearby oil drilling and exploration; there was a group of estancias along the east side of the Andes totaling nearly a million acres threatened by desertification caused by overgrazing.

In the spring of 2001, Kris chartered her own nonprofit, The Patagonia Land Trust, to purchase these wildlands and transfer them to the Argentinean affiliate of the World Wildlife Fund to be administered jointly with the country's national park system. She invited Yvon and me to join the board. Within a year the trust succeeded in acquiring the two properties on the Atlantic coast, the larger of which is named Monte Leon after a prominent headland shaped like a crouching lion, described by Magellan in his log in 1519. With 26 miles of coastline and 16 miles of riverfront, Monte Leon is soon to become Argentina's first coastal national park.

Our next effort is focused on the million acres of grass and steppelands along the east side of the Andes. We are raising money from several sources, including a campaign through Patagonia the company to solicit contributions from its customers in Japan, Europe, and North America; the company is also contributing cash and services to launch the campaign. If successful, it will be the first time a company and its customers have helped to create a national park, and it will be a park that looks like some of the best of Utah, Idaho, and Wyoming put together.

"For 30 years we've profited from the name 'Patagonia'," Yvon said, "and our customers have worn it on their shirts and jackets. So we're encouraging everyone to think of their contribution as a small royalty payment for the usage."

Each year in April, during the austral fall, Kris and Doug return to El Rincon, the estancia at the foot of San Lorenzo. The sheep have been gone for over ten years, and now the native grasses are returning. Doug and Kris follow the same route he, Yvon, and I hiked in 1991, and they camp in the same grove of beech trees under the enormous snow-fluted southeast face of the mountain. And as he did then, each year Doug looks up at the peak and points out to Kris where the route goes.

Last year, when they returned again, Doug sat quietly looking at San Lorenzo, but this time he didn't mention anything about the route.

"You still thinking of climbing it?" Kris asked.

Doug shook his head. "I don't know, Birdy. I think we're too old now."

Then he turned and smiled. "But that's OK. It's good just sitting here looking at it."

Kalasaya Ruins and sunken temple, Tiahuanaco JOHAN REINHARD

sacred landscape ✳ JOHAN REINHARD

The Prehistoric Cultures of the Andes

THE INCA CREATED THE LARGEST EMPIRE in the ancient Americas. In less than a hundred years, they gained control of a region extending over 2,400 miles from their heartland in the highlands of central Peru. Although all Andean cultures lacked writing when the Spanish entered the New World in the middle of the 16th century, the Inca culture became the best known to us today because they were at the height of their power and the Spanish left documents describing their customs and works.

The Inca Empire, however, was the result of cultural developments that had taken place for over two millennia. During that period three cultures particularly stand out: Chavin, Nazca, and

Tiahuanaco. This is primarily due to archaeological remains that have survived to the present day, including massive stonework requiring superior engineering skills and a complex social organization. All three cultures have been considered among the great mysteries of South American archaeology, and fundamental questions remain as to why they built ceremonial structures where they did and what they meant. Recent research points to the sacred landscape as being a key to a better understanding of these cultures.

✳

CHAVIN

IN A REMOTE AREA of the central Peruvian Andes was built a religious center, which was to be one of the most important archaeological sites in South America. The site of Chavin de Huantar especially caught the attention of the Spanish because it clearly predated the Inca, and yet was well constructed and extremely complex, involving an elaborate system of tunnels within a man-made pyramid. Later this center gave its name to a style of iconography that came to be found over a vast area of the central Andes. The Chavin culture lasted about 1,000 years—longer than the Roman Empire.

Chavin de Huantar was one of the largest centers anywhere in the New World at the beginning of the first millennium B.C. Chavin's iconography eventually spread over much of north-central Peru. The site is located on the east side of the Cordillera Blanca at 10,285 feet (3,135 meters) amid rugged mountain terrain. It has been well documented and is visited yearly by thousands of tourists. However, scholars are still unsure what the site meant or even why it was built where it was.

At the time of the Spanish conquest, mountain worship played a prominent role in the religious beliefs of people living near Chavin de Huantar. The most important deity of the people who lived on the west side of the Cordillera Blanca was Huascarán, Peru's highest mountain. An important reason for Chavin's location must have been due to its lying at the foot of one of the highest mountains of the Cordillera Blanca, Huantsan 20,981 feet (6,395 meters). This mountain is near the origin of the Mosna and Santa Rivers, which flow by it on the east and west respectively—one to reach the Pacific Ocean and the other eventually to enter the Amazon and thus to the Atlantic Ocean—making Chavin a geographic and symbolic center with regard to water circulation. Indeed, villagers still make offerings to Huantsan to provide them with water for crops and for the fertility of livestock.

Although the Spanish chroniclers wrote little about religious beliefs and customs in the region of Chavin de Huantar, it is highly likely that Huantsan was the most important mountain worshiped by the people living in its shadow. Huantsan not only is the highest mountain, it dominates the eastern side of the Cordillera Blanca even more than it does the western, where it was regarded as the sacred mountain. Offerings are still being made to Huantsan and other mountains near Chavin to increase the number of livestock and the fertility of crops. For example, in 1945 a lake formed by the melting snow of the Huantsan peaks broke its earthen barrier and swept down the Wacheksa River to flood the Chavin ruins and cover them in mud. Many inhabitants believed that Huantsan caused the flood to stop archaeologists from taking away a famous stone image, the Lanzon.

When viewed in economic terms, the location of Chavin de Huantar might have been selected due to its being located between the coast and tropical forest regions and thus serving as a key point of a trade system, as some scholars have noted. It is situated at one end of the easiest pass through the Cordillera Blanca. Of course, economic functions do not rule out religious ones; mountain deities were (and still are) widely believed to be responsible for success in trade.

Because Chavin de Huantar is situated on the fertile eastern side of the Cordillera Blanca, its location is especially favorable for rainfall agriculture. Thus the area supplies a reasonable subsistence base, while at the same time being at the foot of the highest mountain that is nearest to the origins of the Mosna and Santa Rivers. The Inca noted the religious importance of snow-covered mountains that give origin to rivers, which in turn are used to bring water to the soil. This, of course, has an obvious factual basis, as the quantity and quality of river water are indeed dependent upon snow and rainfall in the mountains. Elaborate channels were built through the ceremonial complex of Chavin so that water originating from the melting snows of Huantsan could be used for ritual purposes. Rivers whose source is a powerful mountain are still widely seen to partake of the mountain's powers, and river confluences, such as found at Chavin, are sacred places in their own right.

The association of mountains, water, and fertility and the persistence of this belief throughout the Andes suggests that a Chavin religious cult spread due to its conforming with religious concepts already held throughout the Andes. This would explain the rapid spread of Chavin iconography, along with a reason why it persisted over such a vast area of the Andes for a millennium—and why it influenced, even if only indirectly, two other great cultures that followed it: Nazca and Tiahuanaco.

Nazca

ONE OF THE BEST KNOWN archaeological sites in South America consists of large figures and lines called geoglyphs drawn on the desert surface near the town of Nazca in southern Peru. The geoglyphs are situated for the most part on the barren plateau between the Ingenio and Nazca River Valleys near the foothills of the Andes. Some of the figures measure over 300 feet in length, and the larger of them can Geoglyphs be seen without distortion only from the air.

Geoglyphs have been found in widely dispersed arid coastal valleys and plains elsewhere in Peru, and numerous geoglyphs have also been found in northern Chile. These were not made by a single culture or in the same time span. Although impressive in other locations, none can rival the geoglyphs found on the desert plain near Nazca in the quantity, variety, size, and elaboration of their forms.

Archaeologists have in broad terms answered the questions as to who made the geoglyphs at Nazca and when. Aside from the dating of potsherds found on the geoglyphs, the approximate ages of some of them can be established based on similarities between them and designs on Nazca pottery with well-established dates. When all the evidence is examined, it is clear that people living in the region of Nazca constructed the geoglyphs sometime between 300 B.C. and about A.D. 700, with some lines possibly being constructed up until the Inca conquest circa A.D. 1475. However, for years no one had a satisfactory explanation as to why they were made.

The actual construction of the geoglyphs was not much of a mystery, as they were formed when stones with oxidized surfaces were removed and the light soil beneath them was exposed. The lack of rain has been a primary reason that they have been able to survive until the present day. Although the plain is crossed by the courses of many dry streams, the placement of the geoglyphs indicates that they were built after the streambeds had formed and that no major climatic changes have occurred since.

Their construction was previously thought to require advanced technology. However, experiments have demonstrated that straight lines could be made by simply using a couple of poles and string and the figures by the extension of a model on the ground and by employing a centerline and locating points by plotting their coordinates.

There is little direct evidence as to the beliefs held by the Nazca people, but archaeological remains, accounts in colonial times of traditional worship, current-day beliefs that are rooted in the past, a study of Nazca iconography, and an examination of the essentially unchanged ecological situation all help in interpreting what these ancient beliefs might have been and how they could have related the geoglyphs to the natural environment and water and fertility. The mountains near Nazca are not the high snow peaks of the central Andes. Nonetheless, the basic beliefs in deities controlling meteorological phenomena appear to have been very similar. Many of these beliefs were held by people living in Nazca in recent times and figure in their legends as well.

Some common elements of these myths should be pointed out. First, they clearly demonstrate that the people of Nazca shared beliefs about the importance of mountain deities in providing water and controlling meteorological phenomena. Second, there is a belief in the ocean as a fertility source, both for the land and for animals. Third, mountains near and distant, high and low in elevation, were important in the beliefs of the Nazca people. Finally, the mountain Tunga was associated with the coast and fertility of fields, and the lower Cerro Blanco—a white mountain of sand—with subterranean water; the high mountains; and the lord of meteorological phenomena, the mountain Illakata. Both Tunga and Cerro Blanco are located near Nazca, and Illakata is linked to Nazca through a river that originates from it.

The only references I have seen made specifically to the *huacas* (sacred places or objects) of the Nazca people at the time of the Spanish conquest were those by the Spanish priests Albornoz and Acosta writing in the late 1500s and Severino's account of 1623. Albornoz mentioned only one huaca for the Nazca people—a mountain. Acosta was told that the principal huaca of the ancient Nazcans was a mountain of sand that stood out amid the stone mountains near Nazca. This could only have been Cerro Blanco. Since Acosta was speaking of ancient Nazcans when he was there, we can assume this mountain was worshiped at least a few centuries earlier—probably the oldest direct evidence of religious beliefs at Nazca that exists.

In an unpublished document of 1623 found in the archbishop's archives of Lima, the priest Severino wrote down the testimonies of people at Nazca concerning traditional religious practices. One man stated that there was no shrine in the village because the people went to worship on a mountain of sand called Moich, on the mountain Huaricangana, and at the springs. Their idols, made of stone, were burned by the Catholic priests. Crosses were placed at all the sites where these idols had been worshiped.

The only mountain of sand near Nazca is Cerro Blanco, whereas Huaricangana (Uracangana or Uracancana on some maps) is today used as the name of one of the summits next to Cerro Tunga, part of the same massif. It appears likely that Huaricangana was the original name for Cerro Tunga. It is no coincidence that mountains and springs were listed together and that they were the most important places of worship of the Nazca people.

Cerro Blanco was believed to have been the wife of Illakata. Cerro Blanco is said to have come down from the highlands to visit the coast, but she failed to return soon enough to her husband. The sun came out and burned her into stone and sand, and she has remained near Nazca to the present day. In this myth we see a linkage of a barren hill near geoglyphs in the desert with a major snow peak of the highlands, and such mountains are still believed to be the principal deities controlling weather and fertility.

Due to the constantly shifting sand, one would not expect to find ruins on Cerro Blanco. However, I did see recent offerings of, among other things, cotton plants and river stones. River stones were, and still are, often used to invoke an increase in the water supply, and the cotton plants were likely placed along with the stones as offerings to gain water for the drought-stricken cotton fields of the Nazca Valley. Cerro Blanco also provides excellent views toward the other principal sacred mountains—Illakata and Tunga.

I observed remains of structures on the summit of Illakata that clearly served a ceremonial purpose. Indeed, several ritual stone mounds appeared to be of recent origin. The archaeological evidence thus supports the legend as to Illakata's ritual importance.

Several pre-Hispanic ritual structures exist on and near the summit of Tunga. Seashells, common offerings for water, were scattered amid some of the ruins. Potsherds were identified as belonging to the late intermediate period (about A.D. 1000-1475), a time when many of the lines were built and used.

Although ethnographic data from Nazca are relatively limited, several anthropologists report that mountain deities are still important for fertility in areas to the east of Nazca. This includes Puquio, 50 miles away, a town with which Nazca has had close contacts for at least several hundred years. Indeed, Puquio provides some of the best information on current-day ceremonies for water and mountain worship. In this town there is a myth about culture heroes who were able to follow the veins of water into the centers of the sacred mountains. Every August ritual specialists climb one of the mountains near Puquio to make offerings for water. The people believe the most important local deities reside in them, that they are responsible for the fertility of livestock in addition to fields, and that the spirits of the dead go to a mountain (Coropuna) to reside. Given the importance of the rains in the mountains and other sources of water for the agriculture of the Nazca people and that the beliefs date at least to Inca times, it seems highly probable that worship of water sources, including mountains both nearby and farther into the Andes, played a prominent role in beliefs at the time the geoglyphs were constructed.

Further evidence supports the association of the Nazca lines with mountain, water, and fertility beliefs. Ethnographic information concerning the use of straight lines in other areas of the Andes demonstrates that they were often related to mountain worship, primarily to obtain water. Of course, these cases do not constitute proof that straight lines were utilized in the same ways at Nazca. However, they at least are in accord with our understanding of Andean beliefs and customs, and they are among the few examples known to date of the traditional use of straight lines.

In Bolivia and in northern Chile, long straight lines frequently lead to hilltops. At Chucuyo in northern Chile, a straight line extends about two and a half miles to the top of a hill. I was told in 1983 that until only a few years previously, worship was made from this point to the surrounding mountains for rain. In Bolivia sacred lines also lead to points from which mountains are worshiped for water.

In Bolivia today lines may belong to individual families or to entire villages, in the sense that they are responsible for their use and upkeep. This could explain why there are so many lines on the plateaus near Nazca and why some cross over others. Over time different groups could have wanted to make their own lines, including making offerings at slightly different points.

The lines were kept straight due to their role as delimiters of sacred space. In Bolivia, those who followed the straight lines were thought to be pardoned for their sins. This would help explain why some of the lines are relatively short or wide; they could have served in these cases not as actual paths, but rather as the sacred space in which worship was performed. Straight lines present a particular problem because of the large number of possible interpretations, both functional and symbolic, that can be offered for them. Most archaeologists agree that the spirals and zigzags played a strictly symbolic role. Spirals were common motifs throughout South America and were frequently used in cults relating to the obtaining of water. The zigzag and oscillating motifs have widely been interpreted as part of a water cult, being thought to represent either rivers or lightning.

Thus the vast majority of figures and lines found at Nazca can be interpreted in terms of a water or fertility cult. Of course, the geoglyphs can be interpreted in many other ways. A substantial body of material exists that enables a theory to be developed relating mountain and fertility beliefs with geoglyphs. This theory allows diverse data to be explained in a logically consistent manner and is in accord with traditional Andean beliefs and practices. One thing at least appears to be clear: Any interpretation of the geoglyphs must take into consideration the ecological situation and the sacred landscape of the region.

The belief that the deities that resided in mountains controlled meteorological phenomena has a sound ecological basis. Sufficient rainfall in the mountains to the east was critical to Nazcan agriculture, either through surface water or the underground water table, which the ancient Nazca people utilized extensively. Ceremonies relating to the worship of deities that controlled weather must have been of prime importance to an agricultural people living in one of the world's most arid regions.

The majority of the lines would likely have served as sacred paths to the places where rituals for fertility were performed; the lines would not have been pointing at anything on the horizon. On the other hand, some lines, especially the large triangles and rectangles, may well have served as symbolic connectors with water sources (rivers, mountains, the ocean) or were sacred areas in which fertility rites were carried out. The various figures, such as birds and whales, would have been formed to invoke water and fertility. Indeed, this is precisely the way that such geoglyphs are interpreted by the traditional inhabitants of northern Chile today. That the figures can be seen best only from the air is explainable as being due to the ability of the mountain deities to oversee the area, such as by appearing as birds or in the form of the mythological flying feline.

One of the reasons that these giant desert geoglyphs have captured so much attention is precisely because there is no simple answer to why they were built. They could have served functions for which we are totally unaware, and they may well have served multiple ends. This does not mean, however, that we cannot come closer to a solution that accords with what we know of traditional Andean beliefs and customs.

✳

TIAHUANACO

THE MONUMENTAL COMPLEX of structures at Tiahuanaco (Tiwanaku), Bolivia, constitutes one of the most impressive archaeological sites in South America. It is situated at 12,615 feet (3,845 meters), about 10 miles to the southeast of Lake Titicaca. Amid an urban center, large monoliths were used in making religious structures nearly 2,000 years ago. This urban-ceremonial complex served as the center for a civilization that lasted nearly a thousand years.

An increase in agricultural production allowed for a surplus that enabled the people to devote time to the construction of the famous temples of Kalasasaya, Akapana, and Pumapunku. Although sites of Tiahuanaco origin are mainly clustered around the eastern half of Lake Titicaca, its influence extended over a considerable distance, including as far west as the Peruvian coast, as far south as the valleys of northern Chile, and beyond Cochabamba in Bolivia to the east.

Tiahuanaco has been extensively documented—in fact, it has become a tourist destination—but why it was built at such a high and barren location and what the structures mean still remains a mystery. Beliefs relating to sacred landscape and mountain and fertility cults appear to hold the key to better understanding Tiahuanaco's location, function, and iconography.

The Tiahuanaco region was no exception to the emphasis on mountain worship, and this continues to be the case to the present. For example, mountains are extremely important among the Callawaya people living to the north of Tiahuanaco. Animals and people are believed to have originated from the mountains at birth and to have returned to them at death. Mountain deities control the fertility of crops, and ritual specialists are considered embodiments of the mountain gods. As elsewhere in the Andes, the mountains are associated with meteorological phenomena.

On the southwest shore of Lake Titicaca the most powerful deities of the region are the high mountains, which also control meteorological phenomena, and worship is still performed today to these mountains for the fertility of crops and animals. Similar beliefs are found on the eastern shore of Lake Titicaca not far from Tiahuanaco. As among the Callawaya, mountains are believed to protect the fields, and ritual specialists chosen by the mountain gods are responsible for preventing hail and for producing rain.

I have witnessed offerings being made to mountain deities on the Island of the Sun in Lake Titicaca. This island was one of the most sacred places in the Inca Empire. Indeed, it was associated with the origin of the Inca in several myths. Today two mountains are of special importance to the local inhabitants: Illampu and Illimani. These two are considered eternal gods and owners of the Earth. At the time of the Spanish conquest, people from the ancient provinces of Lupaqa and Pacajes, which bordered Titicaca to the south and east, believed themselves to be descendants of the marriage between Illampu and Lake Titicaca. Another mountain invoked along with Illampu and Illimani in rites for rain on the Island of the Sun is Sajama, a high, snowcapped peak to the south.

On the Island of the Sun, Illimani and Illampu are superior to all other mountains and even to the deities associated with Lake Titicaca and the Earth, Pachamama. Before making a major offering, the ritual specialist goes to the ancient Inca ruin of Pilcokayna, where he performs divination in a room oriented to the mountain Illampu. He selects the sacred hill on the Island of the Sun on which the offering will be made. The worship is to invoke the mountain gods to protect crops from hail, frost, excess rain, and drought.

Today people living near Tiahuanaco still make offerings to the surrounding mountains, especially the snowcapped peaks such as Illimani, for rain from the summits of the nearby hills. The popular climbing peak of Huayna Potosi 19,985 feet (6,094 meters) also figures prominently in local beliefs. It is the mountain named Cacaaca in an account of 1638 and was widely worshiped in the region of Tiahuanaco, especially to the north, where the Tiahuanaco ruins of Lukurmata and Pajchiri are located. In La Paz, Huayna Potosi is considered to be third in the hierarchy of mountain deities (*achachilas*), behind Illimani and Illampu. Counted among the five most important mountain deities worshiped in Tiahuanaco today, it is particularly believed to be a controller of hail.

Mururata 18,948 feet (5,775 meters) is occasionally invoked at Tiahuanaco as part of fertility rites. In La Paz it is thought to be only behind Illimani, Illampu, and Huayna Potosi in the hierarchy of mountain deities. It is closely associated with Illimani and Sajama in mythology: Mururata's head is said to have been cut off by the weather deity Tunupa after Illimani complained about his actions. It flew off to land and became Sajama.

Weather has been a primary concern of people of this region, since hailstorms have destroyed crops of entire communities, frosts have killed livestock and crops, and violent electrical storms have killed people. Hardly a rainy season passes without lightning causing a death in the vicinity of Tiahuanaco. Nuns living in Colquencha to the southeast told me that lightning killed at least two people a year there, and numerous livestock have died due to lightning as well. I was told in villages east and southeast of Tiahuanaco that people who survived being struck by lightning were viewed as having been selected by a mountain deity to become ritual specialists (*yatiris*).

It is thus no surprise that ceremonies relating to weather control make up an important part of the activities of ritual specialists in the altiplano region. These specialists are believed to gain their power from mountains. On a day-to-day basis ritual specialists most often have to deal with disease and other misfortunes that befall individuals and that also frequently are caused, and cured, by mountain deities. But it is at the community level that the key elements of mountain worship become emphasized. Thus, although mountains may be thought closely associated with a particular meteorological phenomenon, such as hail, all the principal mountains are invoked for good weather and the fertility of crops and livestock.

It is likely that the ceremonial center at Tiahuanaco was primarily concerned with the fertility of plants and animals, especially involving rituals to control meteorological phenomena. But why was it built where it was? Among difficulties such as high altitude and climate was the need to haul huge stone blocks from several miles away. The answer may be primarily due to its relation to four geographical features: the mountains Sajama, Illampu, and Illimani and Lake Titicaca.

Illimani has had such a dominant role in traditional religious beliefs that it is found associated with mountains as distant as Tata Sabaya, some 200 miles to the south. It was the sacred mountain referred to in 1586 as being one of the most widely worshiped deities in this area. This should come as no surprise, for at 17,667 feet (5,385 meters) it is the highest mountain between the ocean to the west and the Amazon Basin to the east. Given its domination of La Paz, it is even less surprising that some 90 percent of the traditional curers in the city have Illimani as their principal traditional deity.

Although not a mountain, Lake Titicaca is a sacred geographical feature that has played, and still plays, an important role in Andean cosmology. In addition to the aquatic resources it supplied, extensive reclamation of land during the Tiahuanaco period from the marshy areas near Lake Titicaca allowed for intensive agricultural production, which provided for a population of some 40,000 people. This land was in turn only available as long as rain, controlled by the weather gods, did not cause the level of Lake Titicaca to rise significantly or the rivers to flood the agricultural land. Indeed, cycles of droughts and flooding of this land may have been a factor in the as yet unexplained decline of Tiahuanaco as a ceremonial center at the end of the first millennium.

During the Inca period, Lake Titicaca was perceived to be an inland sea connected to the ocean, mother of all waters. From its depths emerged the Inca creator deity, Viracocha. People still believe that Lake Titicaca is involved in bringing rain and that it distributes the water sent by the mountain deities.

The lake clearly was of religious importance for the people of Tiahuanaco, as is shown by the majority of their temples having been built near it. Tiahuanaco ritual items have also been found on the Island of the Sun and the Island of the Moon; offerings were found on an underwater ridge near the Island of the Sun. There can be little doubt that Lake Titicaca played a dominant role in Tiahuanaco economic-religious concepts.

Tiahuanaco is built on the only location near a river in a valley connected with Lake Titicaca from which the summit of Illimani is visible, yet also remains in a rough north-south line with the important sacred mountains of Illampu and Sajama. If the site had been built more to the west, this would have placed it in land susceptible to flooding, and if built farther to the east the view to Illimani would have been blocked by lower hills. This location might also explain the orientation of the famous Akapana and Pumapunku pyramidal structures toward Illimani.

The possibility exists that these pyramidal structures represented real or "cosmic" mountains, such as has been hypothesized for pyramids elsewhere in Latin America. This becomes even more likely given that they had elaborate systems for allowing water, held in tanks on their summits, to flow out from them. The tanks could be interpreted as symbolically representing lakes in the mountains, and the channels the rivers. The Akapana is still perceived to be a powerful local protector deity, and offerings continue to be made on its summit to ask it and the great snow mountains, such as Illimani, for whatever is desired. It is compared to being a palace for the mountain gods and believed to have been used for this purpose by the ancient people at Tiahuanaco.

It might be asked, if the mountains were so important, why then have no Tiahuanaco sites been found near them? All of the major mountains invoked at Tiahuanaco are permanently snow-covered and difficult to ascend, even with modern equipment. If Tiahuanaco was in fact built, at least in part, for their worship, then there would be no need to built ceremonial sites closer to them. Pilgrimages to their slopes probably took place and offerings made by communities near them, just as there are today. But these leave few remains.

Tiahuanaco was situated amid the most powerful traditional deities of a vast region, all of which still play important roles with regard to water, weather, and the fertility of crops and animals. Not for nothing was Tiahuanaco considered by traditional peoples to be at the middle of the world at the time of the Spanish conquest. It was located in broad terms at a geographic and symbolic center between the ocean and the Amazonian lowlands. Its specific situation was associated with Lake Titicaca—the largest body of water in the Andes—which was believed to be connected to the ocean—the origin of all water. It was situated in the center of the highest peaks in the region. All these elements taken together make it clear that the site was chosen with care and that it was based on beliefs fundamental to Andean culture.

The belief that deities controlling meteorological phenomena resided in mountains is an ancient concept. Besides being noted in the earliest written records, it is based on ecological facts that would have been clear to anyone living in the Andean region. Mountains do control meteorological phenomena: Rainfall, snow, clouds, lightning, and thunder often originate in the mountains, and they are the sources of the rivers that are so vital to the local economies. Of course, mountains are also physically dominating elements in the natural environment of Andean peoples and form obvious points of contact between earth and sky. Their connection with the underworld, through craters, caves, lakes, and water running beneath the surface, would also not have gone unnoticed. The symbolic significance of a mountain as uniting the three levels of the world—forming an *axis mundi*—is not just confined to the Andes, but is common in many other regions of the world. Mountains have figured prominently in ancient religions. A well-known example, Zeus, the supreme deity of the Greeks, was depicted as residing in a mountain and controlling meteorological phenomena.

In the Andes, the mountain came to be one of the most significant elements in the conceptual system relating to the circulation of water through the subterranean, terrestrial, and celestial spheres. Whatever the initial source of water, the mountain deities were usually the main controllers of it. They thus were the ones who directly affected the crops, animals, and—in the end—

people. The rise of well-organized and complex cultures, such as those of Chavin, Nazca, and Tiahuanaco, led to the construction of ceremonial centers associated with sacred landscape, which included some of the most impressive sites of the ancient world.

When the Inca entered areas where beliefs about mountain worship already existed, they constructed ritual sites relating to it to help in gaining what was, in effect, greater control (political, religious, and economic) over the people and land they conquered. The Inca had compelling reasons to do this: It was their policy not to take food away that the people actually needed and to keep supplies in reserve in case of scarcity. However, they also needed food supplies for the Inca state and religion and thus expanded lands under cultivation wherever they went. It only remained for the Inca to take mountain worship one key step further and to climb to the mountains' summits. Between A.D. 1470 and 1532, the Inca constructed sites on—and made multiple ascensions of—nearly a hundred mountains above 17,000 feet (5,200 meters) and ranging as high as 22,000 feet (6,700 meters). Such heights were not even reached again for four centuries. On these summits they built structures and made offerings that continue to astound.

Waterfall, Oregon PHILIP SCHERMEISTER

the language of animals   ✳   BARRY LOPEZ

THE PRIMARY PURPOSE of the Bloedel Reserve is to create and maintain a place where people can enjoy natural beauty. It is a place to
experience the bond between people and nature. It is a place
in which to enjoy and learn from the emotional and aesthetic
experience of nature the values of harmony, respect for life and
tranquility. It is a place to enjoy and learn the values of eclectic
design, aesthetics and ecology as the catalysts for the harmonious
interaction of people and nature. Consistent with and as a logical
extension to this purpose, The Virginia Merrill Bloedel Lecture
Program was established to recognize and to promote the accomplishments of individuals who have contributed to the welfare of

nature or humanity or to the advancement of science or understanding, that others may learn and benefit by these achievements.

The steep riverine valley I live within, on the west slope of the Cascades in Oregon, has a particular human and natural history. Though I've been here for thirty years, I am able to convey almost none of it. It is not out of inattentiveness. I've wandered widely within the drainages of its eponymous river, the McKenzie; and I could offer you a reasonably complete sketch of its immigrant history, going back to the 1840s. Before then, Tsanchifin Kalapuya, a Penutian-speaking people, camped in these mountains, but they came up the sixty-mile long valley apparently only in summer, to pick berries and to trade with a people living on the far side of the Cascades, the Molala. In the fall, the Tsanchifin returned down valley to winter near present-day Eugene, Oregon, where the McKenzie joins the Willamette River. The Willamette flows a hundred miles north to the Columbia, the Columbia another hundred miles to the Pacific.

The history that preoccupies me, however, in this temperate rain forest is not human history, not even that of the highly integrated Tsanchifin. Native people seem to have left scant trace of their comings and goings in the McKenzie Valley. Only rarely, as I hear it, does someone stumble upon an old, or very old, campsite, where glistening black flakes of a volcanic glass called obsidian, the debitage from tool-making work, turn up in soil scuffed by a boot heel.

I've lingered in such camps, in a respectful and deferential mood, as though the sites were shrines; but I'm drawn more to the woods in which they're found. These landscapes are occupied, still, by the wild animals who were these people's companions. These are the descendants of animals who coursed these woods during the era of the Tsanchifin.

When I travel in the McKenzie basin with visiting friends, my frame of mind is not that of the interpreter, of the cognoscente; I amble with an explorer's temperament, I am alert for the numinous event, for evidence of a world beyond the rational. Though it is presumptuous to say so, I seek a Tsanchifin grasp, the view of an idigene. And what draws me ahead is the possibility of revelation from other indigenes—the testimonies of wild animals.

The idea that animals can convey meaning, and thereby offer an attentive human being illumination, is a commonly held belief the world over. The view is disparaged and disputed only by modern cultures with an allegiance to science as the sole arbiter of truth. The price of this conceit, to my way of thinking, is enormous.

I grew up in a farming valley in southern California in the 1950's, around sheep, dogs, horses, and chickens. The first wild animals I encountered—coyotes, rattlesnakes, mountain lion, deer, and bear—I came upon in the surrounding mountains and deserts. These creatures seemed more vital than domestic animals. They seemed to tremble in the aura of their own light. (I caught a shadow of that magic occasionally in a certain dog, a particular horse, like a residue.) From such a distance it's impossible to recall precisely what riveted my imagination in these encounters, though I might guess. Wild animals are lean. They have no burden of possessions, no need for extra clothing, eating utensils, elaborate dwellings. They are so much more integrated into the landscape than human beings are, swooping its contours and bolting down its pathways with bewildering speed. They travel unerringly through the dark. Holding their gaze, I saw the intensity and clarity I associated with the presence of a soul.

In later years I benefitted from a formal education as a Jesuit prep school in New York City, then at New York University and the universities of Notre Dame and Oregon. I encountered the full range of Western philosophy, including the philosophy of science, in those classrooms and studied the theological foundations of Christianity. I don't feel compelled now to repudiate that instruction. I regard it, though, as incomplete, and would say that nothing I read in those years fundamentally changed what I thought about animals. The more steeped I became in the biology and ecology of animals, the more I understood about migration, and the more I comprehended about the intricacy of their neural impulses and the subtlety of their endocrine systems, the deeper their other unexplored capacities appeared to me. Biochemistry and field studies enhanced rather than diminished my sense that, in Henry Beston's phrase, animals were other nations.

If formal education taught me how to learn something, if it provided me with reliable structures (e.g., *Moby-Dick*, approaching the limit in calculus, von Clausewitz's tactics) within which I could exercise a metaphorical imagination, if the Jesuits inculcated in me a respectful skepticism about authority, then that education gave me the sort of tools most necessary to an examination of the history of Western ideas, a concept fatally flawed by an assumption of progress. I could move on from Gilbert White's Selbourne to Thoreau's Walden. I could trace a thread from Aristotle through Newton at Schrodinger. Or grasp that in the development of symphonic expression, Bach gives way to Mozart who gives way to Beethoven. But this isn't progress. It's change, in a set of ideas that incubate well in our culture.

I left the university with two ideas strong in my mind. One was the belief that a person had to enter the world to know it, that it couldn't be got from a book. The other was that there were other epistemologies out there, as rigorous and valid as the ones I learned in school. Not convinced of the superiority of the latter, I felt ready to consider these other epistemologies, no matter how at odds.

When I moved into the McKenzie valley I saw myself beginning a kind of apprenticeship. Slowly I learned to identify indigenous plants and animals and birds migrating through. Slowly I began to expand the basis of my observations of their lives, to alter the nature of my assumptions. Slowly I began to recognize clusters of life in the valley as opposed to individual, isolated species. I was lucky to live in a place too steep for agriculture to have developed, too heavily wooded to be good for grazing, and too poor in commercial qualities of minerals for mining (though the evidence that all three occurred on a small scale is present.) The only industrial scale impact here has come from commercial logging—and the devastation in parts of the valley is as breathtaking a sight as the napalmed forests of the Vietnam highlands in the 1960's. Pressure is building locally now to develop retirement real estate—trailer parks, RV parks, condominiums; but, for the moment, it's still relatively easy to walk for hours across stretches of land that have never been farmed, logged, mined, graded, or homesteaded. From where my house sits on a wooded bench above the McKenzie River, I can look across the water into a four or five-hundred year old forest in which some of the Douglas firs are more than twenty feet around.

Two ways to "learn" this land are obvious: enter it repeatedly and attentively on your own; or give your attention instead—or alternatively—to its occupants. The most trustworthy occupants, to my mind, are those with no commercial ties, beings whose sense of ownership is guided not by profit but by responsible occupancy. For the valley in which I live, these occupants would theoretically be remnant Tsanchifin people and indigenous animals. To my knowledge, the Tsanchifin are no longer a presence; and the rational mind (to which many of us acquiesce) posits there is little to be learned from animals unless we discover a common language and can converse. This puts the emphasis, I think, in the wrong place. The idea shouldn't be for us to converse, to enter into some sort of Socratic dialogue with animals. It would be to listen to what is already being communicated. To insist on a conversation with the unknown is to demonstrate impatience, and it is to imply that any such encounter must include your being heard.

To know a physical place you must become intimate with it. You must open yourself to its textures, its colors in varying day and night lights, its sonic dimensions. You must in some way become vulnerable to it. In the end, there's little difference between growing into the love of a place and growing into the love of a person. Love matures through intimacy and vulnerability, and it grows most vigorously in an atmosphere of trust. You learn, with regard to the land, the ways in which it is dependable. Where it has no strength to offer you, you do not insist on its support. When you yourself do not understand something, you trust the land might, and you defer.

When I walk in the woods or along the creeks, I'm looking for integration, not conversation. I wasn't to be bound more deeply into the place, to be included, even if only as a witness, in events that animate the landscape. In tracking a mink, in picking a black bear scat apart, in examining red alder trunks deer have scraped with their antlers, I get certain measures of the place where I live. In listening to the songs and tones of Swainson's thrushes and to winter wrens, to the bellows of elk, I get a dimension of the valley I couldn't get on my own. In eating spring chinook, in burning bigleaf maple in the stove, in bathing in ground water from the well, in collecting sorrel and miner's lettuce for a summer salad, I put my life more deeply into the life around me.

The eloquence of animals is in their behavior, not their speech. To see a mule deer stot across a river bar, a sharp-shinned hawk maneuver in dense timber, to watch a female chinook build her nest on clean gravel, to see a rufous hummingbird extracting nectar from foxglove blossoms, to come upon a rubber boa constricting a shrew is to meet the world outside the self. It is to hear the indigenes.

We regard wild creatures as the most animated part of the landscape. We've believed for eons that we share a specific nature with them, different from the nature of wild berries or lightning or water. Our routine exchanges with them are most often simply a verification of this, reaffirmations that we're alive in a particular place together at a particular time.

Wild animals are like us, too, in that they have ancestors. When I see river otter sprawled mid-stream on a boulder in the noon sun, I know their ancestors were here before the fur trappers, before the Tsanchifin, before *Homo*. The same for the cormorant, the woolly bear caterpillar, the cutthroat. In all these histories, in the string of events in each life, the land is revealed. The tensile strength of the orb weaver's silk, the location of the salmon's redd, the shrew-mole's bones bound up in a spotted owl's cast, each makes a concise statement.

Over the years and on several continents I've seen indigenous people enter their landscapes. (I say enter because the landscape of a semi-permanent camp or village, as I have come to understand it, is less intense, less numinous.) Certain aspects of this entry experience seem always to be in evidence. Human conversation usually trails off. People become more curious about animal life, looking at the evidence of what animals have been up to. People begin to look all around, especially behind them, instead of staring straight ahead with only an occasional look to the side. People halt to examine closely things that at first glance seemed innocuous. People stop simply to put things together—the sky with a certain type of forest, a kind of rock outcropping, the sound of a creek, and, last, the droppings of a blue grouse under a thimbleberry bush. People heft rocks and put them back. They push their hands into river mud and perhaps leave patches of it on their skin. It's an on-going intercourse with the place.

Learning one's place through attention to animals is not solely a matter of being open to "statements" they make about the physical, chemical, and biological realms we share. A more profound communication can take place. In this second sphere, animals have volition; they have intention and the power of influence; and they have the capacity to intervene in our lives. I've never known people who were entirely comfortable addressing such things. However we may define "consciousness" in the West, we regard it as a line of demarcation that separates human nature from animal nature. A shaman might cross back and forth, but animals, no.

In my experience indigenous people are most comfortable in asserting a spiritual nature for animals (including aspects of consciousness) only when the purpose of the conversation is to affirm a spirituality shared by both humans and animals. (They're more at ease talking about animals as exemplars of abstract ideals, as oracles and companions, and as metaphorical relations.) When someone relates something previously unheard of that they saw an animal do, something that demonstrates the degree of awareness we call consciousness, the person is saying the world still turns on the miraculous, it's still inventing itself, and that we're a part of this. These observations keep the idea alive that animals are engaged in the world at a deep level.

The fundamental reinforcement of a belief in the spiritual nature of animals' lives (i.e. in the spiritual nature of the landscape itself) comes from a numinous encounter with a wild creature. For many indigenous people (again, in my experience) such events make one feel more secure in the "real" world because their unfolding takes the event beyond the more readily apparent boundaries of existence. In a numinous encounter one's suspicion, profound, persistent, and ineluctable, that there is more to the world than appearances is confirmed. For someone reared in the tradition of the cultural West, it is also a confirmation that Rationalism and the Enlightenment are not points on a continuum of progress but simply two species of wisdom.

Whenever I think of the numinous event, and how vulnerable it is to the pinchers of the analytic mind, I recall a scene in a native village in Alaska. A well-meaning but rude young man, a graduate student in anthropology, had come to this village to study hunting. His ethnocentric interviewing technique was aggressive, his vocabulary academic, his manner to pester and interfere. Day after day he went after people, especially one older man he took to be the best hunter in the village. He hounded him relentlessly, asking him why he was the best hunter. The only way the man could be rid of the interviewer was to answer his question. He ended the assault by saying, "My ability to hunt is like a small bird in my mind. I don't think anyone should disturb it."

A central task facing modern Western cultures is to redefine human community in the wake of industrialization, colonialism and, more recently, the forcing power of capitalism. In trying to solve some of the constellation of attendant problems here—keeping corporations out of secondary education, restoring the physical and spiritual shelter of the family group, preserving non-Western ways of knowing—it seems clear that by cutting ourselves off from nature, by turning nature into scenery and commodities, we may have cut ourselves off from something vital. To repair this damage we can't any longer take what we call "nature" for an object. We must merge it again with our own nature. We must reintegrate ourselves in specific geographic places, and to do that we need to learn those places at a greater depth than any science, Eastern or Western, can take us. We have to incorporate them again in the moral universe we inhabit. We have to develop good relations with them, one that will replace the exploitative relations that have become a defining characteristic of twentieth-century Western life, with its gargantuan oil spills and chemical accidents, its hideous weapons of war, and its conception of wealth that would lead a corporation to cut down a forest to pay the interest on a loan.

In daily conversation in many parts of the American West today, wild animals are given credit for conveying ideas to people, for "speaking". To some degree this is a result of the pervasive influence of Native American culture in certain parts of the West. It doesn't contradict the notion of human intelligence to believe, in these quarters, that wild animals represent repositories of knowledge we've abandoned in our efforts to build civilizations and support ideas like progress and improvement. To "hear" wild animals is not to leave the realm of the human; it's to expand this realm to include voices other than our own. It's a technique for the accomplishment of wisdom. To attend to the language of animals means to give yourself over to a more complicated, less analytic awareness of a place. It's to realize that some of the so-called equations of life are not meant to be solved, that it takes as much intelligence not to solve them as it does to find the putative answers.

A fundamental difference between early and late twentieth-century science in the cultural West has become apparent with the emergence of the phrase "I don't know" in scientific discourse. This admission is the heritage of quantum mechanics. It is heard eloquently today in the talk of cosmologists, plasma physicists, and, increasingly, among field biologists now working beyond the baleful and condescending stare of molecular biologists.

The Enlightenment ideals of an educated mind and just relations among differing people have become problematic in our era because the process of formal education in the West has consistently abjured or condemned non-Western ways of knowing, and because the quest for just relations still strains at the barriers of race, gender, and class. If we truly believe in the wisdom of Enlightenment thought and achievement—and certainly, like Bach's B-Minor Mass, Goethe's theory of light, or Darwin's voyage, that philosophy is among the best we have to offer—then we should consider encouraging the educated mind to wander beyond the comfort of its own solipsisms, and we should extend the principle of justice to include everything that touches our lives.

I do not know how to achieve these things in the small valley where I live except through apprenticeship and the dismantling of assumptions I grew up with. The change, to a more gracious and courteous and wondrous awareness of the world, will not come in my lifetime, and knowing what I know of the modern plagues—oss of biodiversity, global warming, and the individual quest for material wealth—I am fearful. But I believe I have come to whatever I understand by listening to companions and by trying to erase the lines that establish hierarchies of knowledge among them. My sense is that the divine knowledge we yearn for is social, it is not in the province of a genius anymore than it is in the province of a particular culture. It lies within our definition of community.

Our blessing, it seems to me, is not what we know, but that we know each other.

Fitz Roy massif, Patagonia DAVID ANDERSON

lessons from the edge ✳ YVON CHOUINARD

ONE OF THE PROFOUND MEMORIES of my early childhood was of my father sitting in the kitchen next to the wood-burning stove, drinking a bottle of whiskey and pulling out his teeth, both good ones and bad, with his electrician's pliers. He needed dentures but felt the local dentist was asking too much money to do a job he could just as easily do himself.

When I was seven, our family sold our house in the French-speaking town of Lisbon, Maine, and auctioned off all our possessions. The six of us piled into the Chrysler and drove to California. The day after we arrived in Burbank, I was enrolled in public school. Being the smallest boy in class, and unable to speak English, I did the logical thing. On the third day of school, I ran away.

I eventually went back, but ever afterward I remained at the edge of things. Before the other kids in my neighborhood were allowed to cross the street on their own, I was bicycling seven or eight miles to a lake on a private golf course, where I would hide in the willows and fish for bluegills and bass. Later I discovered Griffith Park and the Los Angeles River, where I spent every day after school jigging frogs, trapping crawdads, and hunting cottontails with my bow and arrow.

I didn't take part in any of the usual activities of high school. I remember math class was an opportunity to practice breath holding so, on the weekends, I could free-dive deeper to catch the abundant abalone and lobster off the Malibu coast. A few of us misfits started a falconry club where we used falcons and hawks for hunting. When a 14-year-old kid traps a wild hawk and stays up all night with him until the bird develops enough trust to finally fall asleep on his fist, then trains this proud bird simply with positive reinforcement—well, the Zen master would have to ask, "Just who is getting trained here?"

Rappelling down to falcon aeries led to learning to climb, which led to trips to Wyoming at the age of 16 to climb Gannett Peak, the highest mountain in the Wind River Range. Every year thereafter was spent climbing mountains, kayaking, and fishing rivers. During some of those years I slept 200 days in a sleeping bag. In fact, I resisted buying a tent until I was past 40. I preferred to sleep under the stars or, in storms, under a boulder or tucked under the branches of an alpine fir. I particularly liked sleeping in a hammock hanging from a rock wall on multi-day climbs.

My passion for climbing mountains led to earning a living working as a blacksmith—forging pitons, ice axes, and other tools. I never intended for this craft to become a business, but every time my partner Tom Frost and I returned from the mountains, our heads were spinning with new ideas for improving the existing tools. Our guiding principle of design was a quote from the aviator and writer Antoine St.-Exupéry: "In anything at all, perfection is finally attained not when there is no longer anything to add, but when there is no longer anything to take away." Quality control was always foremost in our minds because if a tool failed it could kill someone.

All winter I forged gear. For the rest of the year, I continued to lead a counter culture life on the fringes of society, living on 50 cents a day on a diet of oatmeal, potatoes, and canned cat food, camping all summer in an old incinerator in the abandoned CCC (Civilian Conservation Corps) camp in the Tetons of Wyoming. In the spring and fall I would climb the granite walls of Yosemite Valley. We were the "Valley Cong," living like guerillas in the nooks and boulders behind Camp 4.

We liked the fact that climbing rocks and icefalls had no economic value for society. We were rebels from the consumer culture of our parents. Businessmen were "grease balls" and corporations were the source of all evil. The natural world was our home. Our heroes were Muir, Thoreau, Emerson, Gaston Rebuffet, and Herman Bühl. We were living on the edges of the ecosystem, adaptable, resilient, and tough. What didn't kill us made us stronger.

We also grew smarter. There's a small river in Jackson Hole, Wyoming, which is solid Class IV or V in high water. It has few eddies in the section that drops 100 feet per mile. I had done this run dozens of times, but one day I decided to do it without a paddle. Now, a kayak paddle is a very powerful tool—perhaps too powerful if it is used in place of technique.

That day I learned to stay low in my boat, keep my weight forward going over drops, look very far ahead, read the river, and follow a natural line. I had to turn my boat by banking and carving rather than depending on a big last-second sweep stroke. My kayaking evolved to another level that day.

From my day in the kayak without a paddle, and other days like it, I learned to appreciate simplicity. Management is the art of organizing complexity. You shouldn't try to solve complex problems with more complexity.

Of course, every winter I returned to my business, even if I didn't call it that. Later on, we applied the same philosophy of simplicity of design and reliability to the production of climbing clothing. The best products are the simplest. Our customers appreciated our "hand-forged" Stand Up Shorts, rugby shirts, and corduroy knickers. It took me 20 years of being in business before I would admit that I was a businessman—and would probably be one for the rest of my life.

The values learned from a life in nature, from climbing and other risk sports, could also be applied to business. In the practice of Zen archery you forget about trying to achieve the goal—that is, hitting the bull's-eye. Instead, you focus on all of the individual movements. You practice your stance, reach back, and pull an arrow out of the quiver, notching it on the string. You match your breathing to the release of the arrow. When you perfect all the elements of shooting an arrow, it can't help but go into the bull's-eye. Climbing mountains, too, is a process. How you climb a mountain is more important than getting to the top.

The process to perfection is through simplification. When T. M. Herbert and I made the first ascent of a route on El Capitan, which we later named the Muir Wall, we studied the route from below, calculated how many days it would take, and took just enough equipment and supplies. Ten days later, we reached the top with no water, food, or bolts left. We knew our abilities, had accurately calculated the risk, and pulled it off. Later, climbers would come and solo the route, free-climb it, do speed ascents. Each generation of climbers has evolved physically and mentally so that equipment becomes less necessary. When the best speed climbers do the 3,000-foot Nose route on El Capitan, they no longer need haul bags or Gore-Tex because they are down by lunch; they may do Half Dome and maybe a couple more walls before the day is over.

Living a life close to nature has also taught me about responsibility. No animal is so stupid and greedy as to foul its own nest—except the human animal. Ten years ago the prestigious Worldwatch Institute reported, "If growth proceeds along the lines of recent decades, it is only a matter of time before global systems collapse under the pressure." Recently, in its State of the World 2000 report, Worldwatch had this to say: "We hoped that we could begin the next century with an upbeat report, one that would show the Earth's health improving. But unfortunately, the list of trends we were concerned with then—shrinking forests, eroding soils, falling water tables, collapsing fisheries, and disappearing species—has since lengthened to include rising temperatures, more destructive storms, dying coral reefs, and melting glaciers."

We are destroying the very systems on which our lives depend. We continue to delude ourselves into thinking that technology is the answer. But technology is a limited tool. It creates industries, but eliminates jobs. It cures disease but doesn't make us healthier. It frees us from some chores but so far has led to a net loss of leisure time. There is a down side to every technological advancement. All technology has really done is to allow more of us to reside on this Earth. Because we are all part of nature, we need to look to nature for the solutions.

To act responsibly, we need to make some fundamental changes. We have to work toward becoming a sustainable society. Planning and decisions need to be made on the premise that we're all going to be around for a long time. The Iroquois nations extended their planning for seven generations into the future. Such planning would preclude natural disasters like clear-cutting the last of the old-growth forests or destroying rivers with dams that will silt up in 20 years. As a businessman, if I really believe in the rightness of such planning, then my own company, which is dependent on nonrenewable resources to make consumer goods, must also do the "right thing."

When I think of sustainability, I think back to when I was a GI in Korea. There I saw farmers pouring night soil on paddies that had been in continuous use for 3,000 years. Each generation of farmers had left the land in as good or better condition as when they received it. Contrast this with modern agribusiness, which wastes two bushels of topsoil to produce one bushel of corn, and pumps groundwater at a rate 25 percent faster than it's being replenished. A responsible government encourages farmers to be good stewards of the land and to practice sustainable agriculture. But why should only the farmer or the fisherman or forester have the responsibility to see that the Earth remains habitable for future generations of humans and other wild things?

My business has taken a close look at its own impact on nature. We do an ongoing environmental assessment of all our business processes, including a "life cycle" analysis of our products—

from fabric source in a field or factory, to manufacturing, to shipping, to consumer cleaning, to ultimate disposal. Then, once you have taken the trouble to learn what you're really doing, you have to act upon that knowledge. We stopped using toxic dyes and found ways to recycle at least 80 percent of our waste materials. We eliminated the use of paper cups, and we reuse paper clips. We use energy-efficient lightbulbs throughout our buildings. We are switching over from recycled paper to paper made from cornstalks, straw, algae, hemp, and kenaf. We now use remilled, used lumber in building our retail stores.

One of the most positive changes was to stop using conventionally grown cotton. Cotton can be one of the most damaging crops to grow on any piece of land. Twenty-five percent of the total insecticide used in the world is applied to cotton fields, which occupy only 3 percent of the world's farmland. Before harvesting, a cotton field is treated up to 25 times with fertilizers, growth promoters, herbicides, pesticides, and fungicides. Then the plant has to be defoliated by mechanical pickers. Arsenic used to be used for this—now paraquat is used, the chemical America used to spray on its wartime enemies. Most of the chemical residue ends up in the aquifer, in workers' lungs, and, since cottonseed is a food product, in your potato chips. When we learned of this in 1995, we decided that we would rather not be in business if we had to make clothing this way. Since 1996 we have not used any industrially grown cotton in our clothing.

We've made some big changes but we've made some disheartening discoveries also. One is that "sustainable manufacturing" is an oxymoron. It's impossible to manufacture something without using more material and energy than the resulting final product. For instance, modern agriculture takes 3,000 calories of fossil fuel to produce a net 1,000 calories of food. The rest is waste. If you wanted to replace the output of one Orlon mill with natural wool, you would have to raise sheep from Maine to the Mississippi. Yet Orlon is made from oil, which is not sustainable. In the long run, any attempt to achieve sustainability on this Earth with six billion people seems doomed to fail. But we have to work toward that goal of sustainability, recognizing that it's an ever-receding summit. It's the process that counts.

These environmental assessments have educated us, and forced us to make hard choices. Each day that we act positively on those choices takes us further along the path to sustainability. Yet we are not martyrs. Every time we elect to do the right thing, it turns out to be more profitable and it strengthens our confidence that we are going to be in business for a long time. That's the lesson corporations need to learn.

But because we realize we're still net polluters, we take another step: We "tax" ourselves for using up nonrenewable resources. We reserve one percent of our total sales or ten percent of our before-tax profits—whichever is greater—and use it to protect and restore our natural environment. Rather than waiting for the government to tax energy consumption and pollution, we decided to do it ourselves. Over the past 15 years Patagonia has contributed more than $15 million to environmental organizations.

Last year we decided to take this idea to the next level: We started an organization called One Percent for the Planet, an alliance of businesses pledging to donate one percent of their net sales to efforts that protect and restore our natural environment. Each member company contributes to organizations of its choosing. This simplifies the decision-making process of the licensing corporation (and minimizes attendant bureaucracy) and encourages member companies to develop independent relationships with the groups they support. In return, member companies are licensed to use the One Percent for the Planet logo in their marketing.

Few believe that it's religious leaders, politicians, or corporate moguls who are going to save us from the apocalyptic slide that we are on when there already exist hundreds of thousands of non-governmental organizations (NGOs) devoted to solving the world's problems. They are far more capable of doing it than multinational corporations or bureaucratic government agencies. The problem is these nonprofits are often dependent on small donations or "bake sales" to fund their good works. The intent of the One Percent for the Planet Alliance is to help fund these diverse environmental organizations so that, collectively, they can be a more powerful force. They can start the revolution.

The one percent idea doesn't have to be limited to businesses. Any individual can do that right now—simply tax yourself. The best part is you decide where the money goes. It's taxation with direct representation, a true democracy. We can all be part of the revolution to transform the way people think.

The importance of environmental action is the most recent lesson that a life on the edge has taught me. All along the way, the natural world forces you to see what you might otherwise miss. Our treasure, all real value, comes from the Earth and sun and it's our responsibility to protect it.

JOHN AMATT was the founder of the Banff Mountain Film Festival in 1976 and was one of the principal organizers and a climber on Canada's first successful expedition to climb Mount Everest.

Born in Lebanon in 1940, BERNARD AMY is a scientist in artificial intelligence and cognitive sciences as well as an accomplished alpinist and traveler. He has authored several books and articles.

DR. EDWIN BERNBAUM is Director of the Sacred Mountains Program at The Mountain Institute and a Research Associate at the University of California at Berkeley. His award-winning book *Sacred Mountains of the World* was the basis for an exhibit of his photography at the Smithsonian Institution.

Founder of Patagonia, Inc., YVON CHOUINARD started in the outdoor business making climbing gear and selling it from his car while making many notable first ascents. He has built a personal and a corporate reputation based on his commitment to reducing our society's environmental impact.

National Geographic Explorer-in-Residence WADE DAVIS is the author of numerous books, including *The Serpent and the Rainbow*, *One River* (1996), and *Light at the Edge of the World* (2002). A native of British Columbia, Davis has conducted ethnographic fieldwork among several indigenous societies of northern Canada.

ED DOUGLAS is the author of *Tenzing: Hero of Everest*, a biography of Tenzing Norgay. Currently associate editor of *Climber* magazine and editor of the *Alpine Journal*, Douglas has authored *Chomolungma Sings the Blues*, and *Regions of the Heart: The Triumph and Tragedy of Alison Hargreaves*, co-written with David Rose.

Winner of the Guggenheim Fellowship and the NEA Creative Writing Fellowship, GRETEL EHRLICH has written many books. Her latest book, *This Cold Heaven: Seven Seasons in Greenland*, illustrates her knowledge and sympathy for the landscape of Greenland, an area she has visited nine times since 1993.

BARRY LOPEZ is the recipient of the National Book Award. His best-known works include *Arctic Dreams* (1986), *Of Wolves and Men* (1978), and *Winter Count* (1981).

Canadian SID MARTY writes on natural history and western life and culture and has published four books of non-fiction and three of poetry, some of which are based on his experiences as a park warden in the Rocky Mountain national parks.

WILLIAM A. McDONOUGH, FAIA, is an internationally renowned designer. *Time* magazine recently recognized him as a "Hero for the Planet," stating that "his utopianism is grounded in a unified philosophy that—in demonstrable and practical ways—is changing the design of the world."

One of the most famous and influential climbers in the world today, REINHOLD MESSNER achieved the first oxygen-free ascent of Everest and was the first man to climb all fourteen 8,000-meter peaks.

CHRIS RAINIER is a leading documentary photographer whose images of sacred places and indigenous peoples have appeared in publications including: *Time, Life,* NATIONAL GEOGRAPHIC, *Outside, Conde Nast Traveler,* the *New York Times, Smithsonian, The New Yorker,* and *French Geo.*

DR. JOHAN REINHARD, a National Geographic Explorer-in-Residence, currently focuses on the sacred beliefs and cultural practices of mountain peoples, especially in the Andes and the Himalaya. During his research in the Andes, he recovered the Inca Ice Maiden on Ampato, chosen by *Time* as one of "the world's ten most important scientific discoveries" of 1995.

RICK RIDGEWAY, in 1978 with three companions, became the first American to reach the summit of K2. He has written five books, including *Below Another Sky,* and is the executive director of the Patagonia Land Trust.

GEORGE B. SCHALLER has contributed to the creation of the Arctic National Wildlife Refuge in Alaska and the Chang Tang Nature Reserve in Tibet, as well as others in Brazil, Pakistan, and Mongolia. His most recent awards include the International Cosmos Prize (Japan) and the Tyler Prize for Environmental Achievement (U.S.A.).

DERMOT SOMERS has over 25 years of climbing and mountaineering experience. His two works of fiction, *Mountains and Other Ghosts* (1990) and *At the Rising of the Moon* (1994), won the Boardman-Tasker Award and Banff Mountain Book Festival award.

DR. JAMES THORSELL is a Senior Advisor for World Heritage at the IUCN (World Conservation Union). His passion for backcountry travel has fueled extensive field missions to over 600 protected areas in 90 countries with more than 150 site evaluations for UNESCO's World Heritage Committee and served as facilitator for the IUCN's Mountain Protected Area Task Force.

Newsweek identified TERRY TEMPEST WILLIAMS as someone likely to make "a considerable impact on the political, economic and environmental issues facing the western states in this decade." Her writing reflects her intimate relationship with the natural world, including *Refuge: An Unnatural History of Place* (1991), *An Unspoken Hunger: Stories from the Field* (1994), and *Desert Quartet* (1995).

BANFF MOUNTAIN SUMMIT

Extreme Landscape: Challenge and Celebration
October 27 - November 3, 2002
Mountain Culture at The Banff Centre, Banff, Alberta, Canada

An event to celebrate the worldwide importance of mountains during the United Nations International Year of Mountains, The Banff Mountain Summit explores how extreme landscape shapes people's lives and how people impact extreme landscape. The authors, scientists, and researchers in this book— men and women who have a passion for mountain places and who have translated that passion into creative endeavors, environmental and scientific research, and critical thinking—are featured at the Summit in Banff.

A global leader in mountain culture and environment, The Banff Centre's Mountain Culture programs empower key voices and effect change in mountain communities around the world. Mountain Culture flagship events— The Banff Mountain Film Festival and Tour, The Banff Mountain Book Festival, and Photography Competition—reach hundreds of thousands of mountain enthusiasts on seven continents. Internationally celebrated for its mountain setting in the Canadian Rockies, innovative programs, world-class conference facilities, and commitment to creative excellence, The Banff Centre is Canada's only learning institution dedicated to the arts, leadership development, and mountain culture. It is located in Canada's first national park and a UNESCO World Heritage site.

The Banff Centre gratefully acknowledges the following sponsors
for their support of this project:

 Parks Canada / Parcs Canada NATIONAL GEOGRAPHIC